Managed M2M Service Providers Complete Self-Assessment Guide

C000060755

The guidance in this Self-Assessment is based on Managed M2M Service Providers best practices and standards in business process architecture, design and quality management. The guidance is also based on the professional judgment of the individual collaborators listed in the Acknowledgments.

Notice of rights

The information in this book is distributed on an "As Is" basis without warranty. While every precaution has been taken in the preparation of he book, neither the author nor the publisher shall have any liability to any person or entity with respect to any loss or damage caused or alleged to be caused directly or indirectly by the instructions contained in this book or by the products described in it.

Trademarks

Many of the designations used by manufacturers and sellers to distinguish their products are claimed as trademarks. Where those designations appear in this book, and the publisher was aware of a trademark claim, the designations appear as requested by the owner of the trademark. All other product names and services identified throughout this book are used in editorial fashion only and for the benefit of such companies with no intention of infringement of the trademark. No such use, or the use of any trade name, is intended to convey endorsement or other affiliation with this book.

Table of Contents

About The Art of Service

The Art of Service, Business Process Architects since 2000, is dedicated to helping stakeholders achieve excellence.

Defining, designing, creating, and implementing a process to solve a stakeholders challenge or meet an objective is the most valuable role... In EVERY group, company, organization and department.

Unless you're talking a one-time, single-use project, there should be a process. Whether that process is managed and implemented by humans, AI, or a combination of the two, it needs to be designed by someone with a complex enough perspective to ask the right questions.

Someone capable of asking the right questions and step back and say, 'What are we really trying to accomplish here? And is there a different way to look at it?'

With The Art of Service's Standard Requirements Self-Assessments, we empower people who can do just that — whether their title is marketer, entrepreneur, manager, salesperson, consultant, Business Process Manager, executive assistant, IT Manager, CIO etc... —they are the people who rule the future. They are people who watch the process as it happens, and ask the right questions to make the process work better.

Contact us when you need any support with this Self-Assessment and any help with templates, blue-prints and examples of standard documents you might need:

http://theartofservice.com
service@theartofservice.com

Included Resources - how to access

Included with your purchase of the book is the Managed M2M

Service Providers Self-Assessment Spreadsheet Dashboard which contains all questions and Self-Assessment areas and auto-generates insights, graphs, and project RACI planning - all with examples to get you started right away.

How? Simply send an email to
access@theartofservice.com
with this books' title in the subject to get the Managed M2M Service Providers Self Assessment Tool right away.

You will receive the following contents with New and Updated specific criteria:

• The latest quick edition of the book in PDF

• The latest complete edition of the book in PDF, which criteria correspond to the criteria in...

• The Self-Assessment Excel Dashboard, and...

• Example pre-filled Self-Assessment Excel Dashboard to get familiar with results generation

• In-depth specific Checklists covering the topic

• Project management checklists and templates to assist with implementation

INCLUDES LIFETIME SELF ASSESSMENT UPDATES

Every self assessment comes with Lifetime Updates and Lifetime Free Updated Books. Lifetime Updates is an industry-first feature which allows you to receive verified self assessment updates, ensuring you always have the most accurate information at your fingertips.

Get it now- you will be glad you did - do it now, before you forget.

Send an email to **access@theartofservice.com** with this books' title in the subject to get the Managed M2M Service Providers Self Assessment Tool right away.

Purpose of this Self-Assessment

This Self-Assessment has been developed to improve understanding of the requirements and elements of Managed M2M Service Providers, based on best practices and standards in business process architecture, design and quality management.

It is designed to allow for a rapid Self-Assessment to determine how closely existing management practices and procedures correspond to the elements of the Self-Assessment.

The criteria of requirements and elements of Managed M2M Service Providers have been rephrased in the format of a Self-Assessment questionnaire, with a seven-criterion scoring system, as explained in this document.

In this format, even with limited background knowledge of Managed M2M Service Providers, a manager can quickly review existing operations to determine how they measure up to the standards. This in turn can serve as the starting point of a 'gap analysis' to identify management tools or system elements that might usefully be implemented in the organization to help improve overall performance.

How to use the Self-Assessment

On the following pages are a series of questions to identify to what extent your Managed M2M Service Providers initiative is complete in comparison to the requirements set in standards.

To facilitate answering the questions, there is a space in front of each question to enter a score on a scale of '1' to '5'.

1 Strongly Disagree

2 Disagree

3 Neutral

4 Agree

5 Strongly Agree

Read the question and rate it with the following in front of mind:

'In my belief,
the answer to this question is clearly defined'.

There are two ways in which you can choose to interpret this statement;
1. how aware are you that the answer to the question is clearly defined
2. for more in-depth analysis you can choose to gather evidence and confirm the answer to the question. This obviously will take more time, most Self-Assessment users opt for the first way to interpret the question and dig deeper later on based on the outcome of the overall Self-Assessment.

A score of '1' would mean that the answer is not clear at all, where a '5' would mean the answer is crystal clear and defined. Leave emtpy when the question is not applicable or you don't want to answer it, you can skip it without affecting your score. Write your score in the space provided.

After you have responded to all the appropriate statements in each section, compute your average score for that section, using the formula provided, and round to the nearest tenth. Then transfer to the corresponding spoke in the Managed M2M Service Providers Scorecard on the second next page of the Self-Assessment.

Your completed Managed M2M Service Providers Scorecard will give you a clear presentation of which Managed M2M Service Providers areas need attention.

Managed M2M Service Providers Scorecard Example

Example of how the finalized Scorecard can look like:

Managed M2M Service Providers Scorecard

Your Scores:

RECOGNIZE

SUSTAIN

DEFINE

CONTROL

MEASURE

IMPROVE

ANALYZE

BEGINNING OF THE SELF-ASSESSMENT:

CRITERION #1: RECOGNIZE

INTENT: Be aware of the need for change. Recognize that there is an unfavorable variation, problem or symptom.

In my belief, the answer to this question is clearly defined:

5 Strongly Agree

4 Agree

3 Neutral

2 Disagree

1 Strongly Disagree

1. Who are your key stakeholders who need to sign off?
<--- Score

2. What problems are you facing and how do you consider Managed M2M service providers will circumvent those obstacles?
<--- Score

3. What does Managed M2M service providers success mean to the stakeholders?

<--- Score

4. What resources or support might you need?

<--- Score

5. Who needs to know about Managed M2M service providers?

<--- Score

6. Are problem definition and motivation clearly presented?

<--- Score

7. What Managed M2M service providers problem should be solved?

<--- Score

8. Do you have/need 24-hour access to key personnel?

<--- Score

9. How are you going to measure success?

<--- Score

10. Does the problem have ethical dimensions?

<--- Score

11. What creative shifts do you need to take?

<--- Score

12. Are employees recognized or rewarded for performance that demonstrates the highest levels of integrity?

<--- Score

13. What would happen if Managed M2M service providers weren't done?
<--- Score

14. Which issues are too important to ignore?
<--- Score

15. Who should resolve the Managed M2M service providers issues?
<--- Score

16. Are there recognized Managed M2M service providers problems?
<--- Score

17. Are employees recognized for desired behaviors?
<--- Score

18. What else needs to be measured?
<--- Score

19. How do you recognize an Managed M2M service providers objection?
<--- Score

20. Have you identified your Managed M2M service providers key performance indicators?
<--- Score

21. What are the stakeholder objectives to be achieved with Managed M2M service providers?
<--- Score

22. Who defines the rules in relation to any given issue?

<--- Score

23. To what extent does each concerned units management team recognize Managed M2M service providers as an effective investment?
<--- Score

24. How much are sponsors, customers, partners, stakeholders involved in Managed M2M service providers? In other words, what are the risks, if Managed M2M service providers does not deliver successfully?
<--- Score

25. Who needs to know?
<--- Score

26. Where is training needed?
<--- Score

27. Are there Managed M2M service providers problems defined?
<--- Score

28. Think about the people you identified for your Managed M2M service providers project and the project responsibilities you would assign to them, what kind of training do you think they would need to perform these responsibilities effectively?
<--- Score

29. Are controls defined to recognize and contain problems?
<--- Score

30. How are training requirements identified?

<--- Score

31. What are the timeframes required to resolve each of the issues/problems?
<--- Score

32. What Managed M2M service providers capabilities do you need?
<--- Score

33. What are the clients issues and concerns?
<--- Score

34. What is the extent or complexity of the Managed M2M service providers problem?
<--- Score

35. Where do you need to exercise leadership?
<--- Score

36. Can management personnel recognize the monetary benefit of Managed M2M service providers?
<--- Score

37. Are there any specific expectations or concerns about the Managed M2M service providers team, Managed M2M service providers itself?
<--- Score

38. For your Managed M2M service providers project, identify and describe the business environment, is there more than one layer to the business environment?
<--- Score

39. What do employees need in the short term?
<--- Score

40. What prevents you from making the changes you know will make you a more effective Managed M2M service providers leader?
<--- Score

41. How do you recognize an objection?
<--- Score

42. Is it needed?
<--- Score

43. What do you need to start doing?
<--- Score

44. What extra resources will you need?
<--- Score

45. How do you identify the kinds of information that you will need?
<--- Score

46. What are the minority interests and what amount of minority interests can be recognized?
<--- Score

47. Would you recognize a threat from the inside?
<--- Score

48. What is the recognized need?
<--- Score

49. Who needs what information?
<--- Score

50. To what extent would your organization benefit from being recognized as a award recipient?
<--- Score

51. As a sponsor, customer or management, how important is it to meet goals, objectives?
<--- Score

52. Why the need?
<--- Score

53. Do you know what you need to know about Managed M2M service providers?
<--- Score

54. What is the Managed M2M service providers problem definition? What do you need to resolve?
<--- Score

55. How are the Managed M2M service providers's objectives aligned to the group's overall stakeholder strategy?
<--- Score

56. Are your goals realistic? Do you need to redefine your problem? Perhaps the problem has changed or maybe you have reached your goal and need to set a new one?
<--- Score

57. How do you take a forward-looking perspective in identifying Managed M2M service providers research related to market response and models?
<--- Score

58. Will Managed M2M service providers deliverables need to be tested and, if so, by whom?
<--- Score

59. Are there regulatory / compliance issues?
<--- Score

60. Are losses recognized in a timely manner?
<--- Score

61. How can auditing be a preventative security measure?
<--- Score

62. Does your organization need more Managed M2M service providers education?
<--- Score

63. Do you need different information or graphics?
<--- Score

64. Will a response program recognize when a crisis occurs and provide some level of response?
<--- Score

65. What are the expected benefits of Managed M2M service providers to the stakeholder?
<--- Score

66. What needs to stay?
<--- Score

67. What should be considered when identifying available resources, constraints, and deadlines?
<--- Score

68. What tools and technologies are needed for a custom Managed M2M service providers project?
<--- Score

69. What are the Managed M2M service providers resources needed?
<--- Score

70. When a Managed M2M service providers manager recognizes a problem, what options are available?
<--- Score

71. Are there any revenue recognition issues?
<--- Score

72. Is the quality assurance team identified?
<--- Score

73. What Managed M2M service providers events should you attend?
<--- Score

74. Why is this needed?
<--- Score

75. Is the need for organizational change recognized?
<--- Score

76. Are you dealing with any of the same issues today as yesterday? What can you do about this?
<--- Score

77. Who else hopes to benefit from it?
<--- Score

78. What vendors make products that address the Managed M2M service providers needs?
<--- Score

79. What is the problem or issue?
<--- Score

80. Who needs budgets?
<--- Score

81. Will it solve real problems?
<--- Score

82. What situation(s) led to this Managed M2M service providers Self Assessment?
<--- Score

83. Whom do you really need or want to serve?
<--- Score

84. What needs to be done?
<--- Score

85. Consider your own Managed M2M service providers project, what types of organizational problems do you think might be causing or affecting your problem, based on the work done so far?
<--- Score

86. How do you identify subcontractor relationships?
<--- Score

87. How does it fit into your organizational needs and tasks?
<--- Score

88. Which information does the Managed M2M service providers business case need to include?
<--- Score

89. What are your needs in relation to Managed M2M service providers skills, labor, equipment, and markets?
<--- Score

90. What is the problem and/or vulnerability?
<--- Score

Add up total points for this section:
_ _ _ _ _ = Total points for this section

Divided by: _ _ _ _ _ _ (number of statements answered) = _ _ _ _ _ _
Average score for this section

Transfer your score to the Managed M2M service providers Index at the beginning of the Self-Assessment.

CRITERION #2: DEFINE:

INTENT: Formulate the stakeholder problem. Define the problem, needs and objectives.

In my belief, the answer to this question is clearly defined:

5 Strongly Agree

4 Agree

3 Neutral

2 Disagree

1 Strongly Disagree

1. How do you manage changes in Managed M2M service providers requirements?
<--- Score

2. What are the boundaries of the scope? What is in bounds and what is not? What is the start point? What is the stop point?
<--- Score

3. What is a worst-case scenario for losses?
<--- Score

4. Do the problem and goal statements meet the SMART criteria (specific, measurable, attainable, relevant, and time-bound)?
<--- Score

5. Are resources adequate for the scope?
<--- Score

6. Scope of sensitive information?
<--- Score

7. What are the Roles and Responsibilities for each team member and its leadership? Where is this documented?
<--- Score

8. How do you catch Managed M2M service providers definition inconsistencies?
<--- Score

9. How do you gather Managed M2M service providers requirements?
<--- Score

10. Has the Managed M2M service providers work been fairly and/or equitably divided and delegated among team members who are qualified and capable to perform the work? Has everyone contributed?
<--- Score

11. Is data collected and displayed to better understand customer(s) critical needs and requirements.

<--- Score

12. Does the scope remain the same?
<--- Score

13. What baselines are required to be defined and managed?
<--- Score

14. Have the customer needs been translated into specific, measurable requirements? How?
<--- Score

15. How do you gather requirements?
<--- Score

16. Has a project plan, Gantt chart, or similar been developed/completed?
<--- Score

17. How do you manage scope?
<--- Score

18. What is the definition of success?
<--- Score

19. What is the worst case scenario?
<--- Score

20. Has a team charter been developed and communicated?
<--- Score

21. What specifically is the problem? Where does it occur? When does it occur? What is its extent?
<--- Score

22. What are the core elements of the Managed M2M service providers business case?
<--- Score

23. Is Managed M2M service providers linked to key stakeholder goals and objectives?
<--- Score

24. What scope to assess?
<--- Score

25. Is the scope of Managed M2M service providers defined?
<--- Score

26. How do you keep key subject matter experts in the loop?
<--- Score

27. Do you have organizational privacy requirements?
<--- Score

28. What are the tasks and definitions?
<--- Score

29. Who defines (or who defined) the rules and roles?
<--- Score

30. The political context: who holds power?
<--- Score

31. What is the context?
<--- Score

32. What is in scope?
<--- Score

33. What was the context?
<--- Score

34. Are there any constraints known that bear on the ability to perform Managed M2M service providers work? How is the team addressing them?
<--- Score

35. Are the Managed M2M service providers requirements testable?
<--- Score

36. Are audit criteria, scope, frequency and methods defined?
<--- Score

37. Do you have a Managed M2M service providers success story or case study ready to tell and share?
<--- Score

38. How do you think the partners involved in Managed M2M service providers would have defined success?
<--- Score

39. What knowledge or experience is required?
<--- Score

40. How have you defined all Managed M2M service providers requirements first?
<--- Score

41. What is the scope of the Managed M2M service providers work?
<--- Score

42. Are different versions of process maps needed to account for the different types of inputs?
<--- Score

43. What critical content must be communicated – who, what, when, where, and how?
<--- Score

44. Is there a critical path to deliver Managed M2M service providers results?
<--- Score

45. Are accountability and ownership for Managed M2M service providers clearly defined?
<--- Score

46. Are approval levels defined for contracts and supplements to contracts?
<--- Score

47. What customer feedback methods were used to solicit their input?
<--- Score

48. Has everyone on the team, including the team leaders, been properly trained?
<--- Score

49. What are the requirements for audit information?
<--- Score

50. If substitutes have been appointed, have they

been briefed on the Managed M2M service providers goals and received regular communications as to the progress to date?
<--- Score

51. What is out-of-scope initially?
<--- Score

52. Will a Managed M2M service providers production readiness review be required?
<--- Score

53. When are meeting minutes sent out? Who is on the distribution list?
<--- Score

54. How was the 'as is' process map developed, reviewed, verified and validated?
<--- Score

55. What Managed M2M service providers requirements should be gathered?
<--- Score

56. Are required metrics defined, what are they?
<--- Score

57. Is there a completed SIPOC representation, describing the Suppliers, Inputs, Process, Outputs, and Customers?
<--- Score

58. What is the definition of Managed M2M service providers excellence?
<--- Score

59. How often are the team meetings?
<--- Score

60. How and when will the baselines be defined?
<--- Score

61. What are the compelling stakeholder reasons for embarking on Managed M2M service providers?
<--- Score

62. What happens if Managed M2M service providers's scope changes?
<--- Score

63. How do you hand over Managed M2M service providers context?
<--- Score

64. Is there a completed, verified, and validated high-level 'as is' (not 'should be' or 'could be') stakeholder process map?
<--- Score

65. Have all of the relationships been defined properly?
<--- Score

66. Are task requirements clearly defined?
<--- Score

67. Who approved the Managed M2M service providers scope?
<--- Score

68. Has the direction changed at all during the course of Managed M2M service providers? If so, when did it

change and why?

<--- Score

69. Is the Managed M2M service providers scope manageable?

<--- Score

70. Have all basic functions of Managed M2M service providers been defined?

<--- Score

71. Is the Managed M2M service providers scope complete and appropriately sized?

<--- Score

72. Where can you gather more information?

<--- Score

73. Is scope creep really all bad news?

<--- Score

74. How will variation in the actual durations of each activity be dealt with to ensure that the expected Managed M2M service providers results are met?

<--- Score

75. Is the current 'as is' process being followed? If not, what are the discrepancies?

<--- Score

76. Is special Managed M2M service providers user knowledge required?

<--- Score

77. How did the Managed M2M service providers manager receive input to the development of a

Managed M2M service providers improvement plan and the estimated completion dates/times of each activity?

<--- Score

78. How do you manage unclear Managed M2M service providers requirements?

<--- Score

79. When is the estimated completion date?

<--- Score

80. How does the Managed M2M service providers manager ensure against scope creep?

<--- Score

81. What constraints exist that might impact the team?

<--- Score

82. Who is gathering information?

<--- Score

83. Is there any additional Managed M2M service providers definition of success?

<--- Score

84. What is in the scope and what is not in scope?

<--- Score

85. Is there regularly 100% attendance at the team meetings? If not, have appointed substitutes attended to preserve cross-functionality and full representation?

<--- Score

86. What is the scope?
<--- Score

87. What key stakeholder process output measure(s) does Managed M2M service providers leverage and how?
<--- Score

88. What are (control) requirements for Managed M2M service providers Information?
<--- Score

89. Is the improvement team aware of the different versions of a process: what they think it is vs. what it actually is vs. what it should be vs. what it could be?
<--- Score

90. How would you define Managed M2M service providers leadership?
<--- Score

91. Why are you doing Managed M2M service providers and what is the scope?
<--- Score

92. What Managed M2M service providers services do you require?
<--- Score

93. How do you build the right business case?
<--- Score

94. What is out of scope?
<--- Score

95. What gets examined?

<--- Score

96. What are the record-keeping requirements of Managed M2M service providers activities?
<--- Score

97. How is the team tracking and documenting its work?
<--- Score

98. Is there a clear Managed M2M service providers case definition?
<--- Score

99. How can the value of Managed M2M service providers be defined?
<--- Score

100. How will the Managed M2M service providers team and the group measure complete success of Managed M2M service providers?
<--- Score

101. Are roles and responsibilities formally defined?
<--- Score

102. Is Managed M2M service providers currently on schedule according to the plan?
<--- Score

103. What are the Managed M2M service providers tasks and definitions?
<--- Score

104. What information do you gather?
<--- Score

105. Who is gathering Managed M2M service providers information?
<--- Score

106. What intelligence can you gather?
<--- Score

107. What are the rough order estimates on cost savings/opportunities that Managed M2M service providers brings?
<--- Score

108. Is there a Managed M2M service providers management charter, including stakeholder case, problem and goal statements, scope, milestones, roles and responsibilities, communication plan?
<--- Score

109. Does the team have regular meetings?
<--- Score

110. In what way can you redefine the criteria of choice clients have in your category in your favor?
<--- Score

111. Is the work to date meeting requirements?
<--- Score

112. What scope do you want your strategy to cover?
<--- Score

113. Is the team adequately staffed with the desired cross-functionality? If not, what additional resources are available to the team?
<--- Score

114. Are there different segments of customers?
<--- Score

115. Has a Managed M2M service providers requirement not been met?
<--- Score

116. What is the scope of Managed M2M service providers?
<--- Score

117. Is Managed M2M service providers required?
<--- Score

118. Has your scope been defined?
<--- Score

119. Are all requirements met?
<--- Score

120. What system do you use for gathering Managed M2M service providers information?
<--- Score

121. What is the scope of the Managed M2M service providers effort?
<--- Score

122. When is/was the Managed M2M service providers start date?
<--- Score

123. Has a high-level 'as is' process map been completed, verified and validated?
<--- Score

124. Who are the Managed M2M service providers improvement team members, including Management Leads and Coaches?
<--- Score

125. Has anyone else (internal or external to the group) attempted to solve this problem or a similar one before? If so, what knowledge can be leveraged from these previous efforts?
<--- Score

126. What would be the goal or target for a Managed M2M service providers's improvement team?
<--- Score

127. How would you define the culture at your organization, how susceptible is it to Managed M2M service providers changes?
<--- Score

128. How are consistent Managed M2M service providers definitions important?
<--- Score

129. What sources do you use to gather information for a Managed M2M service providers study?
<--- Score

130. Has/have the customer(s) been identified?
<--- Score

131. Do you all define Managed M2M service providers in the same way?
<--- Score

132. What information should you gather?

<--- Score

133. What are the Managed M2M service providers use cases?

<--- Score

134. Is it clearly defined in and to your organization what you do?

<--- Score

135. What are the dynamics of the communication plan?

<--- Score

136. How do you gather the stories?

<--- Score

137. What defines best in class?

<--- Score

138. Has the improvement team collected the 'voice of the customer' (obtained feedback – qualitative and quantitative)?

<--- Score

139. Have specific policy objectives been defined?

<--- Score

Add up total points for this section:
_ _ _ _ _ = Total points for this section

Divided by: _ _ _ _ _ _ (number of statements answered) = _ _ _ _ _ _
Average score for this section

Transfer your score to the Managed M2M
service providers Index at the beginning
of the Self-Assessment.

CRITERION #3: MEASURE:

INTENT: Gather the correct data. Measure the current performance and evolution of the situation.

In my belief, the answer to this question is clearly defined:

5 Strongly Agree

4 Agree

3 Neutral

2 Disagree

1 Strongly Disagree

1. What causes extra work or rework?
<--- Score

2. Where is it measured?
<--- Score

3. What is the cost of rework?
<--- Score

4. Do you have an issue in getting priority?
<--- Score

5. What are the Managed M2M service providers investment costs?
<--- Score

6. What is the cause of any Managed M2M service providers gaps?
<--- Score

7. What are allowable costs?
<--- Score

8. Do you have a flow diagram of what happens?
<--- Score

9. Is it possible to estimate the impact of unanticipated complexity such as wrong or failed assumptions, feedback, etcetera on proposed reforms?
<--- Score

10. How to cause the change?
<--- Score

11. Did you tackle the cause or the symptom?
<--- Score

12. What are the Managed M2M service providers key cost drivers?
<--- Score

13. Do you effectively measure and reward individual and team performance?
<--- Score

14. Why do the measurements/indicators matter?
<--- Score

15. Are you aware of what could cause a problem?
<--- Score

16. What users will be impacted?
<--- Score

17. When should you bother with diagrams?
<--- Score

18. How much does it cost?
<--- Score

19. How do you verify and validate the Managed M2M service providers data?
<--- Score

20. What are the costs?
<--- Score

21. How do your measurements capture actionable Managed M2M service providers information for use in exceeding your customers expectations and securing your customers engagement?
<--- Score

22. What measurements are possible, practicable and meaningful?
<--- Score

23. What are your customers expectations and measures?
<--- Score

24. Is there an opportunity to verify requirements?
<--- Score

25. What are the strategic priorities for this year?
<--- Score

26. How will effects be measured?
<--- Score

27. What evidence is there and what is measured?
<--- Score

28. How do you verify your resources?
<--- Score

29. Have design-to-cost goals been established?
<--- Score

30. How is progress measured?
<--- Score

31. What are the costs of delaying Managed M2M service providers action?
<--- Score

32. What do people want to verify?
<--- Score

33. Are Managed M2M service providers vulnerabilities categorized and prioritized?
<--- Score

34. How are costs allocated?
<--- Score

35. What can be used to verify compliance?
<--- Score

36. What causes innovation to fail or succeed in your organization?
<--- Score

37. What are the costs and benefits?
<--- Score

38. What is the Managed M2M service providers business impact?
<--- Score

39. How frequently do you track Managed M2M service providers measures?
<--- Score

40. How do you verify if Managed M2M service providers is built right?
<--- Score

41. What are the costs of reform?
<--- Score

42. Who should receive measurement reports?
<--- Score

43. How sensitive must the Managed M2M service providers strategy be to cost?
<--- Score

44. What are you verifying?
<--- Score

45. What is your Managed M2M service providers

quality cost segregation study?
<--- Score

46. What potential environmental factors impact the Managed M2M service providers effort?
<--- Score

47. What would it cost to replace your technology?
<--- Score

48. Does a Managed M2M service providers quantification method exist?
<--- Score

49. Was a business case (cost/benefit) developed?
<--- Score

50. What measurements are being captured?
<--- Score

51. What causes investor action?
<--- Score

52. How will you measure your Managed M2M service providers effectiveness?
<--- Score

53. How do you quantify and qualify impacts?
<--- Score

54. How can you reduce costs?
<--- Score

55. Who pays the cost?
<--- Score

56. How can you reduce the costs of obtaining inputs?
<--- Score

57. How do you verify the Managed M2M service providers requirements quality?
<--- Score

58. How do you prevent mis-estimating cost?
<--- Score

59. How do you measure variability?
<--- Score

60. Have you made assumptions about the shape of the future, particularly its impact on your customers and competitors?
<--- Score

61. How is the value delivered by Managed M2M service providers being measured?
<--- Score

62. What do you measure and why?
<--- Score

63. Why do you expend time and effort to implement measurement, for whom?
<--- Score

64. What causes mismanagement?
<--- Score

65. What methods are feasible and acceptable to estimate the impact of reforms?
<--- Score

66. How can you measure the performance?
<--- Score

67. What are your key Managed M2M service providers organizational performance measures, including key short and longer-term financial measures?
<--- Score

68. What is the total cost related to deploying Managed M2M service providers, including any consulting or professional services?
<--- Score

69. How do you verify performance?
<--- Score

70. What are your primary costs, revenues, assets?
<--- Score

71. Do you have any cost Managed M2M service providers limitation requirements?
<--- Score

72. How can you manage cost down?
<--- Score

73. What does a Test Case verify?
<--- Score

74. How is performance measured?
<--- Score

75. How do you verify and develop ideas and innovations?
<--- Score

76. Where is the cost?
<--- Score

77. Among the Managed M2M service providers
product and service cost to be estimated, which is
considered hardest to estimate?
<--- Score

78. What drives O&M cost?
<--- Score

79. Which Managed M2M service providers impacts
are significant?
<--- Score

80. What relevant entities could be measured?
<--- Score

81. Do you aggressively reward and promote the
people who have the biggest impact on creating
excellent Managed M2M service providers services/
products?
<--- Score

82. Are you able to realize any cost savings?
<--- Score

83. What does your operating model cost?
<--- Score

84. What are the estimated costs of proposed
changes?
<--- Score

85. Does the Managed M2M service providers task fit

the client's priorities?
<--- Score

86. What is the total fixed cost?
<--- Score

87. Which measures and indicators matter?
<--- Score

88. What harm might be caused?
<--- Score

89. What are the current costs of the Managed M2M service providers process?
<--- Score

90. What details are required of the Managed M2M service providers cost structure?
<--- Score

91. What is an unallowable cost?
<--- Score

92. Are missed Managed M2M service providers opportunities costing your organization money?
<--- Score

93. How will success or failure be measured?
<--- Score

94. What are the uncertainties surrounding estimates of impact?
<--- Score

95. What could cause delays in the schedule?
<--- Score

96. At what cost?
<--- Score

97. Which costs should be taken into account?
<--- Score

98. Are supply costs steady or fluctuating?
<--- Score

99. What are hidden Managed M2M service providers quality costs?
<--- Score

100. What is your decision requirements diagram?
<--- Score

101. Are there any easy-to-implement alternatives to Managed M2M service providers? Sometimes other solutions are available that do not require the cost implications of a full-blown project?
<--- Score

102. How are measurements made?
<--- Score

103. What are the types and number of measures to use?
<--- Score

104. What are the operational costs after Managed M2M service providers deployment?
<--- Score

105. Is the cost worth the Managed M2M service providers effort ?

<--- Score

106. Are the Managed M2M service providers benefits worth its costs?
<--- Score

107. Are the measurements objective?
<--- Score

108. Are you taking your company in the direction of better and revenue or cheaper and cost?
<--- Score

109. How long to keep data and how to manage retention costs?
<--- Score

110. Are there competing Managed M2M service providers priorities?
<--- Score

111. When are costs are incurred?
<--- Score

112. How do you measure success?
<--- Score

113. When a disaster occurs, who gets priority?
<--- Score

114. How will costs be allocated?
<--- Score

115. Are the units of measure consistent?
<--- Score

116. Are there measurements based on task performance?
<--- Score

117. What happens if cost savings do not materialize?
<--- Score

118. What is measured? Why?
<--- Score

119. Are indirect costs charged to the Managed M2M service providers program?
<--- Score

120. What would be a real cause for concern?
<--- Score

121. How do you verify the authenticity of the data and information used?
<--- Score

122. What could cause you to change course?
<--- Score

123. How will measures be used to manage and adapt?
<--- Score

124. What are your operating costs?
<--- Score

125. Will Managed M2M service providers have an impact on current business continuity, disaster recovery processes and/or infrastructure?
<--- Score

126. How will your organization measure success?
<--- Score

127. How do you measure efficient delivery of Managed M2M service providers services?
<--- Score

128. Who is involved in verifying compliance?
<--- Score

129. How can a Managed M2M service providers test verify your ideas or assumptions?
<--- Score

130. What tests verify requirements?
<--- Score

131. Is the solution cost-effective?
<--- Score

132. Do the benefits outweigh the costs?
<--- Score

Add up total points for this section:
_ _ _ _ _ = Total points for this section

Divided by: _ _ _ _ _ _ (number of statements answered) = _ _ _ _ _ _
Average score for this section

Transfer your score to the Managed M2M service providers Index at the beginning of the Self-Assessment.

CRITERION #4: ANALYZE:

INTENT: Analyze causes, assumptions and hypotheses.

In my belief, the answer to this question is clearly defined:

5 Strongly Agree

4 Agree

3 Neutral

2 Disagree

1 Strongly Disagree

1. Were there any improvement opportunities identified from the process analysis?
<--- Score

2. How does the organization define, manage, and improve its Managed M2M service providers processes?
<--- Score

3. What systems/processes must you excel at?

<--- Score

4. Is the suppliers process defined and controlled?
<--- Score

5. What did the team gain from developing a sub-process map?
<--- Score

6. What tools were used to generate the list of possible causes?
<--- Score

7. How is data used for program management and improvement?
<--- Score

8. Where can you get qualified talent today?
<--- Score

9. How do you measure the operational performance of your key work systems and processes, including productivity, cycle time, and other appropriate measures of process effectiveness, efficiency, and innovation?
<--- Score

10. What quality tools were used to get through the analyze phase?
<--- Score

11. How was the detailed process map generated, verified, and validated?
<--- Score

12. How can risk management be tied procedurally to

process elements?

<--- Score

13. Has an output goal been set?

<--- Score

14. Can you add value to the current Managed M2M service providers decision-making process (largely qualitative) by incorporating uncertainty modeling (more quantitative)?

<--- Score

15. How do you use Managed M2M service providers data and information to support organizational decision making and innovation?

<--- Score

16. What qualifications and skills do you need?

<--- Score

17. What are the necessary qualifications?

<--- Score

18. How has the Managed M2M service providers data been gathered?

<--- Score

19. What types of data do your Managed M2M service providers indicators require?

<--- Score

20. What data is gathered?

<--- Score

21. What is the complexity of the output produced?

<--- Score

22. What resources go in to get the desired output?
<--- Score

23. Are you missing Managed M2M service providers opportunities?
<--- Score

24. What Managed M2M service providers data should be collected?
<--- Score

25. What are the disruptive Managed M2M service providers technologies that enable your organization to radically change your business processes?
<--- Score

26. Where is Managed M2M service providers data gathered?
<--- Score

27. How is the way you as the leader think and process information affecting your organizational culture?
<--- Score

28. How do you identify specific Managed M2M service providers investment opportunities and emerging trends?
<--- Score

29. Is there a strict change management process?
<--- Score

30. What do you need to qualify?
<--- Score

31. What, related to, Managed M2M service providers processes does your organization outsource?
<--- Score

32. Identify an operational issue in your organization, for example, could a particular task be done more quickly or more efficiently by Managed M2M service providers?
<--- Score

33. What is the Value Stream Mapping?
<--- Score

34. Is pre-qualification of suppliers carried out?
<--- Score

35. Is the performance gap determined?
<--- Score

36. Who is involved with workflow mapping?
<--- Score

37. What is the oversight process?
<--- Score

38. What qualifications are needed?
<--- Score

39. How often will data be collected for measures?
<--- Score

40. How do your work systems and key work processes relate to and capitalize on your core competencies?

<--- Score

41. Are Managed M2M service providers changes recognized early enough to be approved through the regular process?
<--- Score

42. How will corresponding data be collected?
<--- Score

43. What is your organizations system for selecting qualified vendors?
<--- Score

44. Were any designed experiments used to generate additional insight into the data analysis?
<--- Score

45. What are the personnel training and qualifications required?
<--- Score

46. What Managed M2M service providers data do you gather or use now?
<--- Score

47. What are your Managed M2M service providers processes?
<--- Score

48. What were the financial benefits resulting from any 'ground fruit or low-hanging fruit' (quick fixes)?
<--- Score

49. Are your outputs consistent?
<--- Score

50. When should a process be art not science?
<--- Score

51. Are all staff in core Managed M2M service providers subjects Highly Qualified?
<--- Score

52. Have any additional benefits been identified that will result from closing all or most of the gaps?
<--- Score

53. What qualifies as competition?
<--- Score

54. Should you invest in industry-recognized qualifications?
<--- Score

55. What Managed M2M service providers metrics are outputs of the process?
<--- Score

56. What are the Managed M2M service providers design outputs?
<--- Score

57. Who will facilitate the team and process?
<--- Score

58. Who owns what data?
<--- Score

59. Is data and process analysis, root cause analysis and quantifying the gap/opportunity in place?
<--- Score

60. How do you define collaboration and team output?
<--- Score

61. How do mission and objectives affect the Managed M2M service providers processes of your organization?
<--- Score

62. Think about some of the processes you undertake within your organization, which do you own?
<--- Score

63. What are your key performance measures or indicators and in-process measures for the control and improvement of your Managed M2M service providers processes?
<--- Score

64. What does the data say about the performance of the stakeholder process?
<--- Score

65. What conclusions were drawn from the team's data collection and analysis? How did the team reach these conclusions?
<--- Score

66. Have the problem and goal statements been updated to reflect the additional knowledge gained from the analyze phase?
<--- Score

67. How will the data be checked for quality?
<--- Score

68. Do staff qualifications match your project?
<--- Score

69. How will the change process be managed?
<--- Score

70. Do you have the authority to produce the output?
<--- Score

71. What are your current levels and trends in key measures or indicators of Managed M2M service providers product and process performance that are important to and directly serve your customers? How do these results compare with the performance of your competitors and other organizations with similar offerings?
<--- Score

72. A compounding model resolution with available relevant data can often provide insight towards a solution methodology; which Managed M2M service providers models, tools and techniques are necessary?
<--- Score

73. Who will gather what data?
<--- Score

74. What other organizational variables, such as reward systems or communication systems, affect the performance of this Managed M2M service providers process?
<--- Score

75. Where is the data coming from to measure

compliance?

<--- Score

76. Do your employees have the opportunity to do what they do best everyday?

<--- Score

77. Do quality systems drive continuous improvement?

<--- Score

78. What qualifications are necessary?

<--- Score

79. An organizationally feasible system request is one that considers the mission, goals and objectives of the organization, key questions are: is the Managed M2M service providers solution request practical and will it solve a problem or take advantage of an opportunity to achieve company goals?

<--- Score

80. What output to create?

<--- Score

81. How difficult is it to qualify what Managed M2M service providers ROI is?

<--- Score

82. Do your contracts/agreements contain data security obligations?

<--- Score

83. How is the data gathered?

<--- Score

84. Is there an established change management process?
<--- Score

85. What other jobs or tasks affect the performance of the steps in the Managed M2M service providers process?
<--- Score

86. How are outputs preserved and protected?
<--- Score

87. What are your best practices for minimizing Managed M2M service providers project risk, while demonstrating incremental value and quick wins throughout the Managed M2M service providers project lifecycle?
<--- Score

88. How many input/output points does it require?
<--- Score

89. Who gets your output?
<--- Score

90. Is the final output clearly identified?
<--- Score

91. Was a detailed process map created to amplify critical steps of the 'as is' stakeholder process?
<--- Score

92. What internal processes need improvement?
<--- Score

93. How is the Managed M2M service providers Value

Stream Mapping managed?
<--- Score

94. What are the Managed M2M service providers business drivers?
<--- Score

95. How much data can be collected in the given timeframe?
<--- Score

96. Do several people in different organizational units assist with the Managed M2M service providers process?
<--- Score

97. Do your leaders quickly bounce back from setbacks?
<--- Score

98. What are the processes for audit reporting and management?
<--- Score

99. Are all team members qualified for all tasks?
<--- Score

100. What is the output?
<--- Score

101. Is the required Managed M2M service providers data gathered?
<--- Score

102. What successful thing are you doing today that may be blinding you to new growth

opportunities?

<--- Score

103. How do you ensure that the Managed M2M service providers opportunity is realistic?

<--- Score

104. Who qualifies to gain access to data?

<--- Score

105. What were the crucial 'moments of truth' on the process map?

<--- Score

106. What are your current levels and trends in key Managed M2M service providers measures or indicators of product and process performance that are important to and directly serve your customers?

<--- Score

107. Do you, as a leader, bounce back quickly from setbacks?

<--- Score

108. Did any value-added analysis or 'lean thinking' take place to identify some of the gaps shown on the 'as is' process map?

<--- Score

109. Do you understand your management processes today?

<--- Score

110. Was a cause-and-effect diagram used to explore the different types of causes (or sources of variation)?

<--- Score

111. What is the cost of poor quality as supported by the team's analysis?
<--- Score

112. Has data output been validated?
<--- Score

113. How is Managed M2M service providers data gathered?
<--- Score

114. Is the Managed M2M service providers process severely broken such that a re-design is necessary?
<--- Score

115. What methods do you use to gather Managed M2M service providers data?
<--- Score

116. What training and qualifications will you need?
<--- Score

117. What are your outputs?
<--- Score

118. Have you defined which data is gathered how?
<--- Score

119. What kind of crime could a potential new hire have committed that would not only not disqualify him/her from being hired by your organization, but would actually indicate that he/she might be a particularly good fit?
<--- Score

120. Think about the functions involved in your Managed M2M service providers project, what processes flow from these functions?
<--- Score

121. How do you implement and manage your work processes to ensure that they meet design requirements?
<--- Score

122. What will drive Managed M2M service providers change?
<--- Score

123. What are the best opportunities for value improvement?
<--- Score

124. Were Pareto charts (or similar) used to portray the 'heavy hitters' (or key sources of variation)?
<--- Score

125. What information qualified as important?
<--- Score

126. What is your organizations process which leads to recognition of value generation?
<--- Score

127. Is the gap/opportunity displayed and communicated in financial terms?
<--- Score

128. What process improvements will be needed?
<--- Score

129. What qualifications do Managed M2M service providers leaders need?

<--- Score

130. Which Managed M2M service providers data should be retained?

<--- Score

131. What data do you need to collect?

<--- Score

132. What are the revised rough estimates of the financial savings/opportunity for Managed M2M service providers improvements?

<--- Score

133. What tools were used to narrow the list of possible causes?

<--- Score

Add up total points for this section:
_ _ _ _ _ = Total points for this section

Divided by: _ _ _ _ _ _ (number of statements answered) = _ _ _ _ _ _
Average score for this section

Transfer your score to the Managed M2M service providers Index at the beginning of the Self-Assessment.

CRITERION #5: IMPROVE:

INTENT: Develop a practical solution.
Innovate, establish and test the
solution and to measure the results.

In my belief, the answer to this
question is clearly defined:

5 Strongly Agree

4 Agree

3 Neutral

2 Disagree

1 Strongly Disagree

1. Risk factors: what are the characteristics of
Managed M2M service providers that make it risky?
<--- Score

**2. How do you go about comparing Managed M2M
service providers approaches/solutions?**
<--- Score

3. What lessons, if any, from a pilot were incorporated

into the design of the full-scale solution?
<--- Score

4. Why improve in the first place?
<--- Score

5. What can you do to improve?
<--- Score

6. What are your current levels and trends in key measures or indicators of workforce and leader development?
<--- Score

7. How do you manage Managed M2M service providers risk?
<--- Score

8. What practices helps your organization to develop its capacity to recognize patterns?
<--- Score

9. How do you manage and improve your Managed M2M service providers work systems to deliver customer value and achieve organizational success and sustainability?
<--- Score

10. Was a Managed M2M service providers charter developed?
<--- Score

11. What criteria will you use to assess your Managed M2M service providers risks?
<--- Score

12. Is there a high likelihood that any recommendations will achieve their intended results?
<--- Score

13. Is supporting Managed M2M service providers documentation required?
<--- Score

14. How do you measure risk?
<--- Score

15. What should a proof of concept or pilot accomplish?
<--- Score

16. What are the expected Managed M2M service providers results?
<--- Score

17. What to do with the results or outcomes of measurements?
<--- Score

18. What are the Managed M2M service providers security risks?
<--- Score

19. What is the risk?
<--- Score

20. How is knowledge sharing about risk management improved?
<--- Score

21. How do you decide how much to remunerate an employee?

<--- Score

22. What resources are required for the improvement efforts?
<--- Score

23. What needs improvement? Why?
<--- Score

24. How will you measure the results?
<--- Score

25. How will you know that you have improved?
<--- Score

26. How risky is your organization?
<--- Score

27. How do you mitigate Managed M2M service providers risk?
<--- Score

28. Are events managed to resolution?
<--- Score

29. Is the measure of success for Managed M2M service providers understandable to a variety of people?
<--- Score

30. What went well, what should change, what can improve?
<--- Score

31. Does the goal represent a desired result that can be measured?

<--- Score

32. Who manages supplier risk management in your organization?
<--- Score

33. Are the most efficient solutions problem-specific?
<--- Score

34. Do you have the optimal project management team structure?
<--- Score

35. What tools were used to tap into the creativity and encourage 'outside the box' thinking?
<--- Score

36. Is any Managed M2M service providers documentation required?
<--- Score

37. Is the Managed M2M service providers risk managed?
<--- Score

38. Can you integrate quality management and risk management?
<--- Score

39. Who will be responsible for making the decisions to include or exclude requested changes once Managed M2M service providers is underway?
<--- Score

40. Explorations of the frontiers of Managed M2M service providers will help you build influence,

improve Managed M2M service providers, optimize decision making, and sustain change, what is your approach?

<--- Score

41. What were the criteria for evaluating a Managed M2M service providers pilot?

<--- Score

42. How do you deal with Managed M2M service providers risk?

<--- Score

43. How do you improve Managed M2M service providers service perception, and satisfaction?

<--- Score

44. Are decisions made in a timely manner?

<--- Score

45. If you could go back in time five years, what decision would you make differently? What is your best guess as to what decision you're making today you might regret five years from now?

<--- Score

46. Are risk triggers captured?

<--- Score

47. What improvements have been achieved?

<--- Score

48. How can you improve performance?

<--- Score

49. At what point will vulnerability assessments be

performed once Managed M2M service providers is put into production (e.g., ongoing Risk Management after implementation)?

<--- Score

50. Who are the key stakeholders for the Managed M2M service providers evaluation?

<--- Score

51. Are the key business and technology risks being managed?

<--- Score

52. Where do the Managed M2M service providers decisions reside?

<--- Score

53. Who will be using the results of the measurement activities?

<--- Score

54. Who are the people involved in developing and implementing Managed M2M service providers?

<--- Score

55. What assumptions are made about the solution and approach?

<--- Score

56. What Managed M2M service providers improvements can be made?

<--- Score

57. Will the controls trigger any other risks?

<--- Score

58. What risks do you need to manage?
<--- Score

59. Risk Identification: What are the possible risk events your organization faces in relation to Managed M2M service providers?
<--- Score

60. Can the solution be designed and implemented within an acceptable time period?
<--- Score

61. How is continuous improvement applied to risk management?
<--- Score

62. Who do you report Managed M2M service providers results to?
<--- Score

63. What do you want to improve?
<--- Score

64. What tools do you use once you have decided on a Managed M2M service providers strategy and more importantly how do you choose?
<--- Score

65. How do you keep improving Managed M2M service providers?
<--- Score

66. Are procedures documented for managing Managed M2M service providers risks?
<--- Score

67. What area needs the greatest improvement?
<--- Score

68. Do you cover the five essential competencies: Communication, Collaboration,Innovation, Adaptability, and Leadership that improve an organizations ability to leverage the new Managed M2M service providers in a volatile global economy?
<--- Score

69. How can the phases of Managed M2M service providers development be identified?
<--- Score

70. For decision problems, how do you develop a decision statement?
<--- Score

71. For estimation problems, how do you develop an estimation statement?
<--- Score

72. Who controls the risk?
<--- Score

73. Who will be responsible for documenting the Managed M2M service providers requirements in detail?
<--- Score

74. How are policy decisions made and where?
<--- Score

75. Have you identified breakpoints and/or risk tolerances that will trigger broad consideration of a potential need for intervention or modification of

strategy?
<--- Score

76. Do those selected for the Managed M2M service providers team have a good general understanding of what Managed M2M service providers is all about?
<--- Score

77. Do you need to do a usability evaluation?
<--- Score

78. What tools were used to evaluate the potential solutions?
<--- Score

79. Who manages Managed M2M service providers risk?
<--- Score

80. What strategies for Managed M2M service providers improvement are successful?
<--- Score

81. What is the team's contingency plan for potential problems occurring in implementation?
<--- Score

82. Is the Managed M2M service providers documentation thorough?
<--- Score

83. Do vendor agreements bring new compliance risk ?
<--- Score

84. Is the solution technically practical?

<--- Score

85. Is risk periodically assessed?
<--- Score

86. Are risk management tasks balanced centrally and locally?
<--- Score

87. Which of the recognised risks out of all risks can be most likely transferred?
<--- Score

88. To what extent does management recognize Managed M2M service providers as a tool to increase the results?
<--- Score

89. How do you link measurement and risk?
<--- Score

90. What is Managed M2M service providers risk?
<--- Score

91. What are the implications of the one critical Managed M2M service providers decision 10 minutes, 10 months, and 10 years from now?
<--- Score

92. How do you improve your likelihood of success ?
<--- Score

93. What were the underlying assumptions on the cost-benefit analysis?
<--- Score

94. How will you recognize and celebrate results?
<--- Score

95. How can you improve Managed M2M service providers?
<--- Score

96. How does your organization evaluate strategic Managed M2M service providers success?
<--- Score

97. How scalable is your Managed M2M service providers solution?
<--- Score

98. What are the concrete Managed M2M service providers results?
<--- Score

99. Which Managed M2M service providers solution is appropriate?
<--- Score

100. Risk events: what are the things that could go wrong?
<--- Score

101. Do you combine technical expertise with business knowledge and Managed M2M service providers Key topics include lifecycles, development approaches, requirements and how to make a business case?
<--- Score

102. When you map the key players in your own work and the types/domains of relationships with them,

which relationships do you find easy and which challenging, and why?
<--- Score

103. Can you identify any significant risks or exposures to Managed M2M service providers third- parties (vendors, service providers, alliance partners etc) that concern you?
<--- Score

104. Would you develop a Managed M2M service providers Communication Strategy?
<--- Score

105. What tools were most useful during the improve phase?
<--- Score

106. Are you assessing Managed M2M service providers and risk?
<--- Score

107. What is the magnitude of the improvements?
<--- Score

108. Have you achieved Managed M2M service providers improvements?
<--- Score

109. How will you know when its improved?
<--- Score

110. How can skill-level changes improve Managed M2M service providers?
<--- Score

111. What is the Managed M2M service providers's sustainability risk?

<--- Score

112. How do the Managed M2M service providers results compare with the performance of your competitors and other organizations with similar offerings?

<--- Score

113. How do you define the solutions' scope?

<--- Score

114. Is Managed M2M service providers documentation maintained?

<--- Score

115. Who should make the Managed M2M service providers decisions?

<--- Score

116. What alternative responses are available to manage risk?

<--- Score

117. How do you measure improved Managed M2M service providers service perception, and satisfaction?

<--- Score

118. Where do you need Managed M2M service providers improvement?

<--- Score

119. How can you better manage risk?

<--- Score

120. In the past few months, what is the smallest change you have made that has had the biggest positive result? What was it about that small change that produced the large return?
<--- Score

121. How significant is the improvement in the eyes of the end user?
<--- Score

122. What are the affordable Managed M2M service providers risks?
<--- Score

123. How are Managed M2M service providers risks managed?
<--- Score

124. How do you improve productivity?
<--- Score

125. Does a good decision guarantee a good outcome?
<--- Score

126. What actually has to improve and by how much?
<--- Score

127. Is the scope clearly documented?
<--- Score

128. How will you know that a change is an improvement?
<--- Score

Add up total points for this section:

_____ = Total points for this section

Divided by: _____ (number of
statements answered) = _____
Average score for this section

Transfer your score to the Managed M2M
service providers Index at the beginning
of the Self-Assessment.

CRITERION #6: CONTROL:

INTENT: Implement the practical solution. Maintain the performance and correct possible complications.

In my belief, the answer to this question is clearly defined:

5 Strongly Agree

4 Agree

3 Neutral

2 Disagree

1 Strongly Disagree

1. Is there a transfer of ownership and knowledge to process owner and process team tasked with the responsibilities.
<--- Score

2. Are operating procedures consistent?
<--- Score

3. Do you monitor the Managed M2M service

providers decisions made and fine tune them as they evolve?

<--- Score

4. Are there documented procedures?

<--- Score

5. How will input, process, and output variables be checked to detect for sub-optimal conditions?

<--- Score

6. Against what alternative is success being measured?

<--- Score

7. Is there a control plan in place for sustaining improvements (short and long-term)?

<--- Score

8. How do you plan on providing proper recognition and disclosure of supporting companies?

<--- Score

9. Do the Managed M2M service providers decisions you make today help people and the planet tomorrow?

<--- Score

10. How do senior leaders actions reflect a commitment to the organizations Managed M2M service providers values?

<--- Score

11. How will the process owner and team be able to hold the gains?

<--- Score

12. Is there a standardized process?
<--- Score

13. What is the standard for acceptable Managed M2M service providers performance?
<--- Score

14. Can you adapt and adjust to changing Managed M2M service providers situations?
<--- Score

15. How do you encourage people to take control and responsibility?
<--- Score

16. What are the known security controls?
<--- Score

17. What should the next improvement project be that is related to Managed M2M service providers?
<--- Score

18. What is the control/monitoring plan?
<--- Score

19. Are suggested corrective/restorative actions indicated on the response plan for known causes to problems that might surface?
<--- Score

20. What are you attempting to measure/monitor?
<--- Score

21. Are pertinent alerts monitored, analyzed and

distributed to appropriate personnel?
<--- Score

22. Are controls in place and consistently applied?
<--- Score

23. How do your controls stack up?
<--- Score

24. How can you best use all of your knowledge repositories to enhance learning and sharing?
<--- Score

25. How do controls support value?
<--- Score

26. How will Managed M2M service providers decisions be made and monitored?
<--- Score

27. Is a response plan in place for when the input, process, or output measures indicate an 'out-of-control' condition?
<--- Score

28. What are customers monitoring?
<--- Score

29. Has the improved process and its steps been standardized?
<--- Score

30. How is change control managed?
<--- Score

31. Is knowledge gained on process shared and

institutionalized?
<--- Score

32. What do you stand for--and what are you against?
<--- Score

33. What is the recommended frequency of auditing?
<--- Score

34. Does a troubleshooting guide exist or is it needed?
<--- Score

**35. What are your results for key measures
or indicators of the accomplishment of your
Managed M2M service providers strategy and
action plans, including building and strengthening
core competencies?**
<--- Score

36. What are the key elements of your Managed M2M
service providers performance improvement system,
including your evaluation, organizational learning,
and innovation processes?
<--- Score

37. Who controls critical resources?
<--- Score

**38. What should you measure to verify efficiency
gains?**
<--- Score

39. How might the group capture best practices and
lessons learned so as to leverage improvements?
<--- Score

40. How will new or emerging customer needs/requirements be checked/communicated to orient the process toward meeting the new specifications and continually reducing variation?
<--- Score

41. Are documented procedures clear and easy to follow for the operators?
<--- Score

42. How do you plan for the cost of succession?
<--- Score

43. Has the Managed M2M service providers value of standards been quantified?
<--- Score

44. Are you measuring, monitoring and predicting Managed M2M service providers activities to optimize operations and profitability, and enhancing outcomes?
<--- Score

45. In the case of a Managed M2M service providers project, the criteria for the audit derive from implementation objectives, an audit of a Managed M2M service providers project involves assessing whether the recommendations outlined for implementation have been met, can you track that any Managed M2M service providers project is implemented as planned, and is it working?
<--- Score

46. Will existing staff require re-training, for example, to learn new business processes?
<--- Score

47. What other areas of the group might benefit from the Managed M2M service providers team's improvements, knowledge, and learning?
<--- Score

48. What are the critical parameters to watch?
<--- Score

49. What other systems, operations, processes, and infrastructures (hiring practices, staffing, training, incentives/rewards, metrics/dashboards/scorecards, etc.) need updates, additions, changes, or deletions in order to facilitate knowledge transfer and improvements?
<--- Score

50. Will the team be available to assist members in planning investigations?
<--- Score

51. Is reporting being used or needed?
<--- Score

52. Who has control over resources?
<--- Score

53. Are new process steps, standards, and documentation ingrained into normal operations?
<--- Score

54. What do your reports reflect?
<--- Score

55. Is there documentation that will support the successful operation of the improvement?

<--- Score

56. Is new knowledge gained imbedded in the response plan?
<--- Score

57. Are the planned controls in place?
<--- Score

58. Who is the Managed M2M service providers process owner?
<--- Score

59. Does job training on the documented procedures need to be part of the process team's education and training?
<--- Score

60. What do you measure to verify effectiveness gains?
<--- Score

61. Is there a documented and implemented monitoring plan?
<--- Score

62. How widespread is its use?
<--- Score

63. Does the Managed M2M service providers performance meet the customer's requirements?
<--- Score

64. Is there an action plan in case of emergencies?
<--- Score

65. What is the best design framework for Managed M2M service providers organization now that, in a post industrial-age if the top-down, command and control model is no longer relevant?
<--- Score

66. What can you control?
<--- Score

67. How will the day-to-day responsibilities for monitoring and continual improvement be transferred from the improvement team to the process owner?
<--- Score

68. Is there a Managed M2M service providers Communication plan covering who needs to get what information when?
<--- Score

69. What key inputs and outputs are being measured on an ongoing basis?
<--- Score

70. Is a response plan established and deployed?
<--- Score

71. Who will be in control?
<--- Score

72. Have new or revised work instructions resulted?
<--- Score

73. Who is going to spread your message?
<--- Score

74. Will your goals reflect your program budget?
<--- Score

75. Is there a recommended audit plan for routine surveillance inspections of Managed M2M service providers's gains?
<--- Score

76. Is the Managed M2M service providers test/monitoring cost justified?
<--- Score

77. Do you monitor the effectiveness of your Managed M2M service providers activities?
<--- Score

78. Will any special training be provided for results interpretation?
<--- Score

79. How will the process owner verify improvement in present and future sigma levels, process capabilities?
<--- Score

80. Can support from partners be adjusted?
<--- Score

81. How is Managed M2M service providers project cost planned, managed, monitored?
<--- Score

82. What Managed M2M service providers standards are applicable?
<--- Score

83. What is your theory of human motivation, and

how does your compensation plan fit with that view?
<--- Score

84. What adjustments to the strategies are needed?
<--- Score

85. You may have created your quality measures at a time when you lacked resources, technology wasn't up to the required standard, or low service levels were the industry norm. Have those circumstances changed?
<--- Score

86. What quality tools were useful in the control phase?
<--- Score

87. Are the Managed M2M service providers standards challenging?
<--- Score

88. Are the planned controls working?
<--- Score

89. How do you establish and deploy modified action plans if circumstances require a shift in plans and rapid execution of new plans?
<--- Score

90. How will report readings be checked to effectively monitor performance?
<--- Score

91. How will you measure your QA plan's effectiveness?
<--- Score

92. Does Managed M2M service providers appropriately measure and monitor risk?
<--- Score

93. How do you spread information?
<--- Score

94. Who sets the Managed M2M service providers standards?
<--- Score

95. Does the response plan contain a definite closed loop continual improvement scheme (e.g., plan-do-check-act)?
<--- Score

96. How likely is the current Managed M2M service providers plan to come in on schedule or on budget?
<--- Score

97. How do you select, collect, align, and integrate Managed M2M service providers data and information for tracking daily operations and overall organizational performance, including progress relative to strategic objectives and action plans?
<--- Score

98. What is your plan to assess your security risks?
<--- Score

Add up total points for this section:
_ _ _ _ _ = Total points for this section

Divided by: _ _ _ _ _ _ (number of

statements answered) = _ _ _ _ _ _
Average score for this section

Transfer your score to the Managed M2M
service providers Index at the beginning
of the Self-Assessment.

CRITERION #7: SUSTAIN:

INTENT: Retain the benefits.

In my belief, the answer to this
question is clearly defined:

5 Strongly Agree

4 Agree

3 Neutral

2 Disagree

1 Strongly Disagree

1. How are you doing compared to your industry?
<--- Score

**2. What are the essentials of internal Managed
M2M service providers management?**
<--- Score

**3. If you find that you havent accomplished one of
the goals for one of the steps of the Managed M2M
service providers strategy, what will you do to fix
it?**

<--- Score

4. Think of your Managed M2M service providers project, what are the main functions?
<--- Score

5. What relationships among Managed M2M service providers trends do you perceive?
<--- Score

6. Who do you want your customers to become?
<--- Score

7. Why not do Managed M2M service providers?
<--- Score

8. What is a feasible sequencing of reform initiatives over time?
<--- Score

9. Is maximizing Managed M2M service providers protection the same as minimizing Managed M2M service providers loss?
<--- Score

10. Who are four people whose careers you have enhanced?
<--- Score

11. Are the criteria for selecting recommendations stated?
<--- Score

12. What is it like to work for you?
<--- Score

13. Is your basic point _____ or _____?
<--- Score

14. Will it be accepted by users?
<--- Score

15. How do you stay inspired?
<--- Score

16. Why should people listen to you?
<--- Score

17. What counts that you are not counting?
<--- Score

18. What are the long-term Managed M2M service providers goals?
<--- Score

19. What are the top 3 things at the forefront of your Managed M2M service providers agendas for the next 3 years?
<--- Score

20. Is a Managed M2M service providers team work effort in place?
<--- Score

21. How can you incorporate support to ensure safe and effective use of Managed M2M service providers into the services that you provide?
<--- Score

22. What happens if you do not have enough funding?
<--- Score

23. What does your signature ensure?
<--- Score

24. Are you paying enough attention to the partners your company depends on to succeed?
<--- Score

25. If you had to rebuild your organization without any traditional competitive advantages (i.e., no killer technology, promising research, innovative product/ service delivery model, etcetera), how would your people have to approach their work and collaborate together in order to create the necessary conditions for success?
<--- Score

26. Who will provide the final approval of Managed M2M service providers deliverables?
<--- Score

27. Who do we want your customers to become?
<--- Score

28. How do you transition from the baseline to the target?
<--- Score

29. Is it economical; do you have the time and money?
<--- Score

30. Are you / should you be revolutionary or evolutionary?
<--- Score

31. Where can you break convention?

<--- Score

32. In a project to restructure Managed M2M service providers outcomes, which stakeholders would you involve?
<--- Score

33. What is the purpose of Managed M2M service providers in relation to the mission?
<--- Score

34. Can the schedule be done in the given time?
<--- Score

35. In the past year, what have you done (or could you have done) to increase the accurate perception of your company/brand as ethical and honest?
<--- Score

36. Would you rather sell to knowledgeable and informed customers or to uninformed customers?
<--- Score

37. How do you create buy-in?
<--- Score

38. Are assumptions made in Managed M2M service providers stated explicitly?
<--- Score

39. How do you maintain Managed M2M service providers's Integrity?
<--- Score

40. What should you stop doing?

<--- Score

41. How do you ensure that implementations of Managed M2M service providers products are done in a way that ensures safety?
<--- Score

42. Marketing budgets are tighter, consumers are more skeptical, and social media has changed forever the way we talk about Managed M2M service providers, how do you gain traction?
<--- Score

43. Is Managed M2M service providers realistic, or are you setting yourself up for failure?
<--- Score

44. When information truly is ubiquitous, when reach and connectivity are completely global, when computing resources are infinite, and when a whole new set of impossibilities are not only possible, but happening, what will that do to your business?
<--- Score

45. What will be the consequences to the stakeholder (financial, reputation etc) if Managed M2M service providers does not go ahead or fails to deliver the objectives?
<--- Score

46. How do you make it meaningful in connecting Managed M2M service providers with what users do day-to-day?
<--- Score

47. What potential megatrends could make your

business model obsolete?

<--- Score

48. To whom do you add value?

<--- Score

49. What may be the consequences for the performance of an organization if all stakeholders are not consulted regarding Managed M2M service providers?

<--- Score

50. Do you feel that more should be done in the Managed M2M service providers area?

<--- Score

51. What is the estimated value of the project?

<--- Score

52. Are you changing as fast as the world around you?

<--- Score

53. Do you think you know, or do you know you know ?

<--- Score

54. Can you do all this work?

<--- Score

55. How do senior leaders deploy your organizations vision and values through your leadership system, to the workforce, to key suppliers and partners, and to customers and other stakeholders, as appropriate?

<--- Score

56. What is the craziest thing you can do?
<--- Score

57. What Managed M2M service providers skills are most important?
<--- Score

58. How do you keep records, of what?
<--- Score

59. Will there be any necessary staff changes (redundancies or new hires)?
<--- Score

60. Whose voice (department, ethnic group, women, older workers, etc) might you have missed hearing from in your company, and how might you amplify this voice to create positive momentum for your business?
<--- Score

61. How do you accomplish your long range Managed M2M service providers goals?
<--- Score

62. Do you have the right capabilities and capacities?
<--- Score

63. What is your Managed M2M service providers strategy?
<--- Score

64. Is there any existing Managed M2M service providers governance structure?

<--- Score

65. Who are your customers?
<--- Score

66. What are you trying to prove to yourself, and how might it be hijacking your life and business success?
<--- Score

67. What is the source of the strategies for Managed M2M service providers strengthening and reform?
<--- Score

68. How do you foster innovation?
<--- Score

69. What management system can you use to leverage the Managed M2M service providers experience, ideas, and concerns of the people closest to the work to be done?
<--- Score

70. What information is critical to your organization that your executives are ignoring?
<--- Score

71. What is the recommended frequency of auditing?
<--- Score

72. What one word do you want to own in the minds of your customers, employees, and partners?
<--- Score

73. How do you govern and fulfill your societal responsibilities?
<--- Score

74. What did you miss in the interview for the worst hire you ever made?
<--- Score

75. What current systems have to be understood and/or changed?
<--- Score

76. What you are going to do to affect the numbers?
<--- Score

77. What are the gaps in your knowledge and experience?
<--- Score

78. How do you engage the workforce, in addition to satisfying them?
<--- Score

79. Who else should you help?
<--- Score

80. Who, on the executive team or the board, has spoken to a customer recently?
<--- Score

81. What trophy do you want on your mantle?
<--- Score

82. Are your responses positive or negative?
<--- Score

83. What is the overall talent health of your organization as a whole at senior levels, and for

each organization reporting to a member of the Senior Leadership Team?
<--- Score

84. Who will be responsible for deciding whether Managed M2M service providers goes ahead or not after the initial investigations?
<--- Score

85. Ask yourself: how would you do this work if you only had one staff member to do it?
<--- Score

86. What are the performance and scale of the Managed M2M service providers tools?
<--- Score

87. Why do and why don't your customers like your organization?
<--- Score

88. Which individuals, teams or departments will be involved in Managed M2M service providers?
<--- Score

89. Operational - will it work?
<--- Score

90. How do you know if you are successful?
<--- Score

91. What unique value proposition (UVP) do you offer?
<--- Score

92. What is the overall business strategy?

<--- Score

93. Who have you, as a company, historically been when you've been at your best?
<--- Score

94. Is Managed M2M service providers dependent on the successful delivery of a current project?
<--- Score

95. How will you motivate the stakeholders with the least vested interest?
<--- Score

96. Why will customers want to buy your organizations products/services?
<--- Score

97. What are the success criteria that will indicate that Managed M2M service providers objectives have been met and the benefits delivered?
<--- Score

98. If you do not follow, then how to lead?
<--- Score

99. Who is responsible for ensuring appropriate resources (time, people and money) are allocated to Managed M2M service providers?
<--- Score

100. If no one would ever find out about your accomplishments, how would you lead differently?
<--- Score

101. What could happen if you do not do it?

<--- Score

102. If you got fired and a new hire took your place, what would she do different?
<--- Score

103. Has implementation been effective in reaching specified objectives so far?
<--- Score

104. What are strategies for increasing support and reducing opposition?
<--- Score

105. At what moment would you think; Will I get fired?
<--- Score

106. Are you making progress, and are you making progress as Managed M2M service providers leaders?
<--- Score

107. What are your personal philosophies regarding Managed M2M service providers and how do they influence your work?
<--- Score

108. What role does communication play in the success or failure of a Managed M2M service providers project?
<--- Score

109. What are specific Managed M2M service providers rules to follow?
<--- Score

110. What stupid rule would you most like to kill?

<--- Score

111. What have been your experiences in defining long range Managed M2M service providers goals?
<--- Score

112. What are the challenges?
<--- Score

113. How do you manage Managed M2M service providers Knowledge Management (KM)?
<--- Score

114. What is your BATNA (best alternative to a negotiated agreement)?
<--- Score

115. What are the barriers to increased Managed M2M service providers production?
<--- Score

116. What are your most important goals for the strategic Managed M2M service providers objectives?
<--- Score

117. Who is responsible for errors?
<--- Score

118. What is the kind of project structure that would be appropriate for your Managed M2M service providers project, should it be formal and complex, or can it be less formal and relatively simple?
<--- Score

119. How important is Managed M2M service providers to the user organizations mission?

<--- Score

120. Which models, tools and techniques are necessary?
<--- Score

121. How can you become the company that would put you out of business?
<--- Score

122. What goals did you miss?
<--- Score

123. Are all key stakeholders present at all Structured Walkthroughs?
<--- Score

124. Why should you adopt a Managed M2M service providers framework?
<--- Score

125. Who is the main stakeholder, with ultimate responsibility for driving Managed M2M service providers forward?
<--- Score

126. How much contingency will be available in the budget?
<--- Score

127. Why is Managed M2M service providers important for you now?
<--- Score

128. Who is responsible for Managed M2M service providers?

<--- Score

129. How do you provide a safe environment -physically and emotionally?
<--- Score

130. What knowledge, skills and characteristics mark a good Managed M2M service providers project manager?
<--- Score

131. What are the potential basics of Managed M2M service providers fraud?
<--- Score

132. Why is it important to have senior management support for a Managed M2M service providers project?
<--- Score

133. Who is on the team?
<--- Score

134. What are internal and external Managed M2M service providers relations?
<--- Score

135. How do you determine the key elements that affect Managed M2M service providers workforce satisfaction, how are these elements determined for different workforce groups and segments?
<--- Score

136. What trouble can you get into?
<--- Score

137. How do customers see your organization?
<--- Score

138. What have you done to protect your business from competitive encroachment?
<--- Score

139. What happens when a new employee joins the organization?
<--- Score

140. What must you excel at?
<--- Score

141. What is the funding source for this project?
<--- Score

142. What threat is Managed M2M service providers addressing?
<--- Score

143. Whom among your colleagues do you trust, and for what?
<--- Score

144. Is the Managed M2M service providers organization completing tasks effectively and efficiently?
<--- Score

145. Who do you think the world wants your organization to be?
<--- Score

146. How do you set Managed M2M service providers stretch targets and how do you get

people to not only participate in setting these stretch targets but also that they strive to achieve these?

<--- Score

147. How will you insure seamless interoperability of Managed M2M service providers moving forward?

<--- Score

148. If you were responsible for initiating and implementing major changes in your organization, what steps might you take to ensure acceptance of those changes?

<--- Score

149. Are you maintaining a past–present–future perspective throughout the Managed M2M service providers discussion?

<--- Score

150. Do you have past Managed M2M service providers successes?

<--- Score

151. Is a Managed M2M service providers breakthrough on the horizon?

<--- Score

152. Which Managed M2M service providers goals are the most important?

<--- Score

153. What would have to be true for the option on the table to be the best possible choice?

<--- Score

154. How is implementation research currently incorporated into each of your goals?
<--- Score

155. How will you ensure you get what you expected?
<--- Score

156. What is your competitive advantage?
<--- Score

157. Do you think Managed M2M service providers accomplishes the goals you expect it to accomplish?
<--- Score

158. What are current Managed M2M service providers paradigms?
<--- Score

159. How do you go about securing Managed M2M service providers?
<--- Score

160. What is an unauthorized commitment?
<--- Score

161. What are the short and long-term Managed M2M service providers goals?
<--- Score

162. How do you keep the momentum going?
<--- Score

163. What is something you believe that nearly no one agrees with you on?
<--- Score

164. What are the key enablers to make this Managed M2M service providers move?
<--- Score

165. What projects are going on in the organization today, and what resources are those projects using from the resource pools?
<--- Score

166. What happens at your organization when people fail?
<--- Score

167. What are the rules and assumptions your industry operates under? What if the opposite were true?
<--- Score

168. What business benefits will Managed M2M service providers goals deliver if achieved?
<--- Score

169. How do you track customer value, profitability or financial return, organizational success, and sustainability?
<--- Score

170. What Managed M2M service providers modifications can you make work for you?
<--- Score

171. What are the business goals Managed M2M service providers is aiming to achieve?
<--- Score

172. What was the last experiment you ran?

<--- Score

173. Who will determine interim and final deadlines?
<--- Score

174. How do you foster the skills, knowledge, talents, attributes, and characteristics you want to have?
<--- Score

175. What is your question? Why?
<--- Score

176. Which functions and people interact with the supplier and or customer?
<--- Score

177. What new services of functionality will be implemented next with Managed M2M service providers ?
<--- Score

178. What is the range of capabilities?
<--- Score

Add up total points for this section:
_ _ _ _ _ = Total points for this section

Divided by: _ _ _ _ _ _ (number of statements answered) = _ _ _ _ _ _
Average score for this section

Transfer your score to the Managed M2M service providers Index at the beginning of the Self-Assessment.

Managed M2M Service Providers and Managing Projects, Criteria for Project Managers:

1.0 Initiating Process Group: Managed M2M Service Providers

1. How will you do it?

2. Do you know the roles & responsibilities required for this Managed M2M Service Providers project?

3. Did the Managed M2M Service Providers project team have the right skills?

4. Do you know if the Managed M2M Service Providers project requires outside equipment or vendor resources?

5. When must it be done?

6. Do you understand the communication expectations for this Managed M2M Service Providers project?

7. What are the overarching issues of your organization?

8. Who is funding the Managed M2M Service Providers project?

9. How will you know you did it?

10. What were things that you did well, and could improve, and how?

11. Who are the Managed M2M Service Providers project stakeholders?

12. What business situation is being addressed?

13. During which stage of Risk planning are modeling techniques used to determine overall effects of risks on Managed M2M Service Providers project objectives for high probability, high impact risks?

14. Are you properly tracking the progress of the Managed M2M Service Providers project and communicating the status to stakeholders?

15. How well did the chosen processes produce the expected results?

16. How well did the chosen processes fit the needs of the Managed M2M Service Providers project?

17. How should needs be met?

18. Were sponsors and decision makers available when needed outside regularly scheduled meetings?

19. How well defined and documented were the Managed M2M Service Providers project management processes you chose to use?

20. Where must it be done?

1.1 Project Charter: Managed M2M Service Providers

21. What are the constraints?

22. Must Have?

23. Who manages integration?

24. Who ise input and support will this Managed M2M Service Providers project require?

25. Pop quiz – which are the same inputs as in the Managed M2M Service Providers project charter?

26. What ideas do you have for initial tests of change (PDSA cycles)?

27. Why have you chosen the aim you have set forth?

28. For whom?

29. Who are the stakeholders?

30. What is in it for you?

31. How do you manage integration?

32. Is time of the essence?

33. When will this occur?

34. Why use a Managed M2M Service Providers

project charter?

35. What are you striving to accomplish (measurable goal(s))?

36. Why do you need to manage scope?

37. When?

38. How will you know that a change is an improvement?

39. What are the assigned resources?

40. What changes can you make to improve?

1.2 Stakeholder Register: Managed M2M Service Providers

41. How much influence do they have on the Managed M2M Service Providers project?

42. What is the power of the stakeholder?

43. Is your organization ready for change?

44. What & Why?

45. How big is the gap?

46. How should employers make voices heard?

47. Who is managing stakeholder engagement?

48. How will reports be created?

49. What are the major Managed M2M Service Providers project milestones requiring communications or providing communications opportunities?

50. Who wants to talk about Security?

51. What opportunities exist to provide communications?

1.3 Stakeholder Analysis Matrix: Managed M2M Service Providers

52. Inoculations or payment to receive them?

53. Resources, assets, people?

54. Cashflow, start-up cash-drain?

55. New USPs?

56. Industry or lifestyle trends?

57. What do you need to appraise?

58. What is the stakeholders mandate, what is mission?

59. What are the reimbursement requirements?

60. What is your Risk Management?

61. Do the stakeholders goals and expectations support or conflict with the Managed M2M Service Providers project goals?

62. How affected by the problem(s)?

63. New markets, vertical, horizontal?

64. What do people from other organizations see as your organizations weaknesses?

65. What are the key services, contractual arrangements, or other relationships between stakeholder groups?

66. Are there people who ise voices or interests in the issue may not be heard?

67. What tools would help you communicate?

68. Competitive advantages?

69. Would it be fair to say that cost is a controlling criteria?

70. Who will be affected by the work?

71. Who can contribute financial or technical resources towards the work?

2.0 Planning Process Group: Managed M2M Service Providers

72. What will you do?

73. In what way has the program contributed towards the issue culture and development included on the public agenda?

74. Professionals want to know what is expected from them; what are the deliverables?

75. Is the Managed M2M Service Providers project making progress in helping to achieve the set results?

76. How well do the team follow the chosen processes?

77. Who are the Managed M2M Service Providers project stakeholders?

78. Explanation: is what the Managed M2M Service Providers project intents to solve a hard question?

79. Did you read it correctly?

80. Have more efficient (sensitive) and appropriate measures been adopted to respond to the political and socio-cultural problems identified?

81. What factors are contributing to progress or delay in the achievement of products and results?

82. Is the identification of the problems, inequalities and gaps, with respective causes, clear in the Managed M2M Service Providers project?

83. Why do it Managed M2M Service Providers projects fail?

84. How will it affect you?

85. Will you be replaced?

86. How are it Managed M2M Service Providers projects different?

87. To what extent do the intervention objectives and strategies of the Managed M2M Service Providers project respond to your organizations plans?

88. Does it make any difference if you are successful?

89. What is the NEXT thing to do?

90. What type of estimation method are you using?

2.1 Project Management Plan: Managed M2M Service Providers

91. Are there any Client staffing expectations?

92. How do you organize the costs in the Managed M2M Service Providers project management plan?

93. Has the selected plan been formulated using cost effectiveness and incremental analysis techniques?

94. What is the justification?

95. Is there an incremental analysis/cost effectiveness analysis of proposed mitigation features based on an approved method and using an accepted model?

96. Is mitigation authorized or recommended?

97. What would you do differently?

98. When is a Managed M2M Service Providers project management plan created?

99. Do the proposed changes from the Managed M2M Service Providers project include any significant risks to safety?

100. Why do you manage integration?

101. What data/reports/tools/etc. do your PMs need?

102. Is there anything you would now do differently

on your Managed M2M Service Providers project based on past experience?

103. Are calculations and results of analyzes essentially correct?

104. Where does all this information come from?

105. Are there non-structural buyout or relocation recommendations?

106. What worked well?

107. Will you add a schedule and diagram?

108. What went wrong?

2.2 Scope Management Plan: Managed M2M Service Providers

109. Is stakeholder involvement adequate?

110. How many changes are you making?

111. Describe the process for rejecting the Managed M2M Service Providers project deliverables. What happens to rejected deliverables?

112. Is the schedule updated on a periodic basis?

113. Does all Managed M2M Service Providers project documentation reside in a common repository for easy access?

114. Does the implementation plan have an appropriate division of responsibilities?

115. Are risk oriented checklists used during risk identification?

116. Are the results of quality assurance reviews provided to affected groups & individuals?

117. Are vendor contract reports, reviews and visits conducted periodically?

118. Is each item clearly and completely defined?

119. What are the acceptance criteria (process and criteria to be met for key stakeholder acceptance) and

who is authorized to sign off?

120. Are written status reports provided on a designated frequent basis?

121. Are Managed M2M Service Providers project leaders committed to this Managed M2M Service Providers project full time?

122. Does the business case include how the Managed M2M Service Providers project aligns with your organizations strategic goals & objectives?

123. Are mitigation strategies identified?

124. Have Managed M2M Service Providers project management standards and procedures been identified / established and documented?

125. Are there any windfall benefits that would accrue to the Managed M2M Service Providers project sponsor or other parties?

126. Has the budget been baselined?

127. How relevant is this attribute to this Managed M2M Service Providers project or audit?

128. Are estimating assumptions and constraints captured?

2.3 Requirements Management Plan: Managed M2M Service Providers

129. Who will do the reporting and to whom will reports be delivered?

130. What is the earliest finish date for this Managed M2M Service Providers project if it is scheduled to start on ...?

131. How often will the reporting occur?

132. Do you have an appropriate arrangement for meetings?

133. Will the Managed M2M Service Providers project requirements become approved in writing?

134. What cost metrics will be used?

135. Is infrastructure setup part of your Managed M2M Service Providers project?

136. How will unresolved questions be handled once approval has been obtained?

137. Is the system software (non-operating system) new to the IT Managed M2M Service Providers project team?

138. Should you include sub-activities?

139. Will you use tracing to help understand the

impact of a change in requirements?

140. What information regarding the Managed M2M Service Providers project requirements will be reported?

141. How will requirements be managed?

142. Controlling Managed M2M Service Providers project requirements involves monitoring the status of the Managed M2M Service Providers project requirements and managing changes to the requirements. Who is responsible for monitoring and tracking the Managed M2M Service Providers project requirements?

143. If it exists, where is it housed?

144. Do you have price sheets and a methodology for determining the total proposal cost?

145. Has the requirements team been instructed in the Change Control process?

146. Who is responsible for quantifying the Managed M2M Service Providers project requirements?

147. Is there formal agreement on who has authority to approve a change in requirements?

148. Is the system software (non-operating system) new to the IT Managed M2M Service Providers project team?

2.4 Requirements Documentation: Managed M2M Service Providers

149. What are the attributes of a customer?

150. What will be the integration problems?

151. Has requirements gathering uncovered information that would necessitate changes?

152. Does the system provide the functions which best support the customers needs?

153. The problem with gathering requirements is right there in the word gathering. What images does it conjure?

154. What marketing channels do you want to use: e-mail, letter or sms?

155. How much does requirements engineering cost?

156. Where do you define what is a customer, what are the attributes of customer?

157. What is the risk associated with the technology?

158. What happens when requirements are wrong?

159. How can you document system requirements?

160. What kind of entity is a problem ?

161. Completeness. are all functions required by the customer included?

162. Where are business rules being captured?

163. What if the system wasn t implemented?

164. Is your business case still valid?

165. Verifiability. can the requirements be checked?

166. Who provides requirements?

167. Can the requirements be checked?

168. What is a show stopper in the requirements?

2.5 Requirements Traceability Matrix: Managed M2M Service Providers

169. How small is small enough?

170. What percentage of Managed M2M Service Providers projects are producing traceability matrices between requirements and other work products?

171. How will it affect the stakeholders personally in career?

172. Why use a WBS?

173. Describe the process for approving requirements so they can be added to the traceability matrix and Managed M2M Service Providers project work can be performed. Will the Managed M2M Service Providers project requirements become approved in writing?

174. Will you use a Requirements Traceability Matrix?

175. Is there a requirements traceability process in place?

176. Why do you manage scope?

177. Do you have a clear understanding of all subcontracts in place?

178. How do you manage scope?

179. What are the chronologies, contingencies,

consequences, criteria?

180. What is the WBS?

2.6 Project Scope Statement: Managed M2M Service Providers

181. Is the plan under configuration management?

182. Have you been able to thoroughly document the Managed M2M Service Providers projects assumptions and constraints?

183. Identify how your team and you will create the Managed M2M Service Providers project scope statement and the work breakdown structure (WBS). Document how you will create the Managed M2M Service Providers project scope statement and WBS, and make sure you answer the following questions: In defining Managed M2M Service Providers project scope and the WBS, will you and your Managed M2M Service Providers project team be using methods defined by your organization, methods defined by the Managed M2M Service Providers project management office (PMO), or other methods?

184. Have you been able to easily identify success criteria and create objective measurements for each of the Managed M2M Service Providers project scopes goal statements?

185. Is the scope of your Managed M2M Service Providers project well defined?

186. Risks?

187. Will there be a Change Control Process in place?

188. Who will you recommend approve the change, and when do you recommend the change reviews occur?

189. Is there a Change Management Board?

190. Will the risk documents be filed?

191. Have the configuration management functions been assigned?

192. Write a brief purpose statement for this Managed M2M Service Providers project. Include a business justification statement. What is the product of this Managed M2M Service Providers project?

193. Once its defined, what is the stability of the Managed M2M Service Providers project scope?

194. What process would you recommend for creating the Managed M2M Service Providers project scope statement?

195. Is there an information system for the Managed M2M Service Providers project?

196. Will tasks be marked complete only after QA has been successfully completed?

197. Is the Managed M2M Service Providers project sponsor function identified and defined?

198. Are there adequate Managed M2M Service Providers project control systems?

199. Is the change control process documented and on file?

200. What are the defined meeting materials?

2.7 Assumption and Constraint Log: Managed M2M Service Providers

201. How are new requirements or changes to requirements identified?

202. What does an audit system look like?

203. Security analysis has access to information that is sanitized?

204. Are formal code reviews conducted?

205. Are there ways to reduce the time it takes to get something approved?

206. Are there nonconformance issues?

207. Model-building: what data-analytic strategies are useful when building proportional-hazards models?

208. Is there a Steering Committee in place?

209. Does the plan conform to standards?

210. Has a Managed M2M Service Providers project Communications Plan been developed?

211. Does the traceability documentation describe the tool and/or mechanism to be used to capture traceability throughout the life cycle?

212. What weaknesses do you have?

213. Are there procedures in place to effectively manage interdependencies with other Managed M2M Service Providers projects / systems?

214. What is positive about the current process?

215. Have you eliminated all duplicative tasks or manual efforts, where appropriate?

216. What other teams / processes would be impacted by changes to the current process, and how?

217. After observing execution of process, is it in compliance with the documented Plan?

218. How many Managed M2M Service Providers project staff does this specific process affect?

219. What strengths do you have?

220. Are there processes defining how software will be developed including development methods, overall timeline for development, software product standards, and traceability?

2.8 Work Breakdown Structure: Managed M2M Service Providers

221. How will you and your Managed M2M Service Providers project team define the Managed M2M Service Providers projects scope and work breakdown structure?

222. Is it still viable?

223. Who has to do it?

224. Do you need another level?

225. When do you stop?

226. What is the probability of completing the Managed M2M Service Providers project in less that xx days?

227. What is the probability that the Managed M2M Service Providers project duration will exceed xx weeks?

228. When does it have to be done?

229. Can you make it?

230. Why would you develop a Work Breakdown Structure?

231. Why is it useful?

232. Is the work breakdown structure (wbs) defined and is the scope of the Managed M2M Service Providers project clear with assigned deliverable owners?

233. How far down?

234. Where does it take place?

235. How many levels?

236. How big is a work-package?

2.9 WBS Dictionary: Managed M2M Service Providers

237. Can the contractor substantiate work package and planning package budgets?

238. Does the scheduling system provide for the identification of work progress against technical and other milestones, and also provide for forecasts of completion dates of scheduled work?

239. Does the sum of all work package budgets plus planning packages within control accounts equal the budgets assigned to the already stated control accounts?

240. Detailed schedules which support control account and work package start and completion dates/events?

241. Wbs elements contractually specified for reporting of status to you (lowest level only)?

242. Does the contractors system provide unit costs, equivalent unit or lot costs in terms of labor, material, other direct, and indirect costs?

243. Are work packages assigned to performing organizations?

244. Budgeted cost for work performed?

245. Are Managed M2M Service Providers projected

overhead costs in each pool and the associated direct costs used as the basis for establishing interim rates for allocating overhead to contracts?

246. Performance to date and material commitment?

247. Do the lines of authority for incurring indirect costs correspond to the lines of responsibility for management control of the same components of costs?

248. Are the bases and rates for allocating costs from each indirect pool to commercial work consistent with the already stated used to allocate corresponding costs to Government contracts?

249. Are estimates developed by Managed M2M Service Providers project personnel coordinated with the already stated responsible for overall management to determine whether required resources will be available according to revised planning?

250. Is cost and schedule performance measurement done in a consistent, systematic manner?

251. Are retroactive changes to BCWS and BCWP prohibited except for correction of errors or for normal accounting adjustments?

252. Does the contractors system provide for determination of price variance by comparing planned Vs actual commitments?

253. Major functional areas of contract effort?

254. What size should a work package be?

255. Is the entire contract planned in time-phased control accounts to the extent practicable?

2.10 Schedule Management Plan: Managed M2M Service Providers

256. Are changes in scope (deliverable commitments) agreed to by all affected groups & individuals?

257. Why conduct schedule analysis?

258. Are right task and resource calendars used in the IMS?

259. Have Managed M2M Service Providers project team accountabilities & responsibilities been clearly defined?

260. Have all necessary approvals been obtained?

261. Are all attributes of the activities defined, including risk and uncertainty?

262. Are milestone deliverables effectively tracked and compared to Managed M2M Service Providers project plan?

263. Have all involved Managed M2M Service Providers project stakeholders and work groups committed to the Managed M2M Service Providers project?

264. Are all vendor contracts closed out?

265. Is current scope of the Managed M2M Service Providers project substantially different than that

originally defined?

266. Will rolling way planning be used?

267. Is Managed M2M Service Providers project status reviewed with the steering and executive teams at appropriate intervals?

268. Are decisions captured in a decisions log?

269. Is the steering committee active in Managed M2M Service Providers project oversight?

270. Are internal Managed M2M Service Providers project status meetings held at reasonable intervals?

271. Are the schedule estimates reasonable given the Managed M2M Service Providers project?

272. Is there an approved case?

273. Have reserves been created to address risks?

274. Are any non-compliance issues that exist due to your organizations practices communicated to your organization?

275. Have adequate resources been provided by management to ensure Managed M2M Service Providers project success?

2.11 Activity List: Managed M2M Service Providers

276. Are the required resources available or need to be acquired?

277. How should ongoing costs be monitored to try to keep the Managed M2M Service Providers project within budget?

278. What is the total time required to complete the Managed M2M Service Providers project if no delays occur?

279. What will be performed?

280. What is your organizations history in doing similar activities?

281. How difficult will it be to do specific activities on this Managed M2M Service Providers project?

282. How can the Managed M2M Service Providers project be displayed graphically to better visualize the activities?

283. What are the critical bottleneck activities?

284. In what sequence?

285. How detailed should a Managed M2M Service Providers project get?

286. What is the LF and LS for each activity?

287. Is infrastructure setup part of your Managed M2M Service Providers project?

288. For other activities, how much delay can be tolerated?

289. How do you determine the late start (LS) for each activity?

290. The wbs is developed as part of a joint planning session. and how do you know that youhave done this right?

291. How much slack is available in the Managed M2M Service Providers project?

292. When do the individual activities need to start and finish?

293. How will it be performed?

294. What is the probability the Managed M2M Service Providers project can be completed in xx weeks?

2.12 Activity Attributes: Managed M2M Service Providers

295. Activity: what is Missing?

296. Which method produces the more accurate cost assignment?

297. Is there anything planned that does not need to be here?

298. Have constraints been applied to the start and finish milestones for the phases?

299. What activity do you think you should spend the most time on?

300. Time for overtime?

301. Has management defined a definite timeframe for the turnaround or Managed M2M Service Providers project window?

302. Why?

303. Do you feel very comfortable with your prediction?

304. Can more resources be added?

305. How else could the items be grouped?

306. How many days do you need to complete the

work scope with a limit of X number of resources?

307. Were there other ways you could have organized the data to achieve similar results?

308. How many resources do you need to complete the work scope within a limit of X number of days?

309. How difficult will it be to complete specific activities on this Managed M2M Service Providers project?

310. What is missing?

311. Where else does it apply?

312. Resource is assigned to?

2.13 Milestone List: Managed M2M Service Providers

313. How will the milestone be verified?

314. How difficult will it be to do specific activities on this Managed M2M Service Providers project?

315. Loss of key staff?

316. Legislative effects?

317. Vital contracts and partners?

318. What specific improvements did you make to the Managed M2M Service Providers project proposal since the previous time?

319. What date will the task finish?

320. Who will manage the Managed M2M Service Providers project on a day-to-day basis?

321. What would happen if a delivery of material was one week late?

322. Own known vulnerabilities?

323. Global influences?

324. What are your competitors vulnerabilities?

325. Sustaining internal capabilities?

326. How will you get the word out to customers?

327. How late can each activity be finished and started?

328. Information and research?

329. How soon can the activity start?

330. Describe the industry you are in and the market growth opportunities. What is the market for your technology, product or service?

331. Insurmountable weaknesses?

2.14 Network Diagram: Managed M2M Service Providers

332. Where do schedules come from?

333. Review the logical flow of the network diagram. Take a look at which activities you have first and then sequence the activities. Do they make sense?

334. Can you calculate the confidence level?

335. What can be done concurrently?

336. Are you on time?

337. How difficult will it be to do specific activities on this Managed M2M Service Providers project?

338. If a current contract exists, can you provide the vendor name, contract start, and contract expiration date?

339. Why must you schedule milestones, such as reviews, throughout the Managed M2M Service Providers project?

340. Will crashing x weeks return more in benefits than it costs?

341. If the Managed M2M Service Providers project network diagram cannot change and you have extra personnel resources, what is the BEST thing to do?

342. What activity must be completed immediately before this activity can start?

343. What must be completed before an activity can be started?

344. How confident can you be in your milestone dates and the delivery date?

345. Exercise: what is the probability that the Managed M2M Service Providers project duration will exceed xx weeks?

346. What are the Key Success Factors?

347. What activities must follow this activity?

348. If x is long, what would be the completion time if you break x into two parallel parts of y weeks and z weeks?

349. What are the Major Administrative Issues?

350. Are the gantt chart and/or network diagram updated periodically and used to assess the overall Managed M2M Service Providers project timetable?

2.15 Activity Resource Requirements: Managed M2M Service Providers

351. Which logical relationship does the PDM use most often?

352. How do you manage time?

353. Do you use tools like decomposition and rolling-wave planning to produce the activity list and other outputs?

354. How do you handle petty cash?

355. Anything else?

356. When does monitoring begin?

357. Are there unresolved issues that need to be addressed?

358. Why do you do that?

359. What is the Work Plan Standard?

360. What are constraints that you might find during the Human Resource Planning process?

361. Organizational Applicability?

362. Other support in specific areas?

363. How many signatures do you require on a

check and does this match what is in your policy and procedures?

2.16 Resource Breakdown Structure: Managed M2M Service Providers

364. When do they need the information?

365. Goals for the Managed M2M Service Providers project. What is each stakeholders desired outcome for the Managed M2M Service Providers project?

366. How difficult will it be to do specific activities on this Managed M2M Service Providers project?

367. What is each stakeholders desired outcome for the Managed M2M Service Providers project?

368. Why do you do it?

369. Which resources should be in the resource pool?

370. How can this help you with team building?

371. Who is allowed to see what data about which resources?

372. Who delivers the information?

373. Who is allowed to perform which functions?

374. What is the difference between % Complete and % work?

375. What is the purpose of assigning and documenting responsibility?

376. What is the number one predictor of a groups productivity?

377. Why is this important?

378. Who will be used as a Managed M2M Service Providers project team member?

379. How should the information be delivered?

380. What is the primary purpose of the human resource plan?

381. What defines a successful Managed M2M Service Providers project?

2.17 Activity Duration Estimates: Managed M2M Service Providers

382. Do procedures exist that identify when and how human resources are introduced and removed from the Managed M2M Service Providers project?

383. Is earned value analysis completed to assess Managed M2M Service Providers project performance?

384. Is a work breakdown structure created to organize and to confirm the scope of each Managed M2M Service Providers project?

385. Which includes asking team members about the time estimates for activities and reaching agreement on the calendar date for each activity?

386. Will the new application be developed using existing hardware, software, and networks?

387. Who will be the main sponsor for it?

388. Will the new application negatively affect the current IT infrastructure?

389. How do theories relate to Managed M2M Service Providers project management?

390. What is involved in the solicitation process?

391. Are team building activities completed to

improve team performance?

392. What is the BEST thing for the Managed M2M Service Providers project manager to do?

393. Does a process exist to determine the probability of risk events?

394. Under corresponding circumstances what would be the best thing to do?

395. When would a milestone chart be used instead of a bar char?

396. Are updates on work results collected and used as inputs to the performance reporting process?

397. Is action taken to increase the effectiveness and efficiency of Managed M2M Service Providers projects?

398. Are the causes of all variances identified?

399. Describe a Managed M2M Service Providers project that suffered from scope creep. Could it have been avoided?

400. How could you define throughput and how would your organization benefit from maximizing it?

2.18 Duration Estimating Worksheet: Managed M2M Service Providers

401. Is this operation cost effective?

402. Small or large Managed M2M Service Providers project?

403. What is your role?

404. What is the total time required to complete the Managed M2M Service Providers project if no delays occur?

405. Science = process: remember the scientific method?

406. What utility impacts are there?

407. What is cost and Managed M2M Service Providers project cost management?

408. Can the Managed M2M Service Providers project be constructed as planned?

409. Is the Managed M2M Service Providers project responsive to community need?

410. Will the Managed M2M Service Providers project collaborate with the local community and leverage resources?

411. Why estimate time and cost?

412. What is next?

413. Value pocket identification & quantification what are value pockets?

414. How can the Managed M2M Service Providers project be displayed graphically to better visualize the activities?

415. Done before proceeding with this activity or what can be done concurrently?

416. How should ongoing costs be monitored to try to keep the Managed M2M Service Providers project within budget?

2.19 Project Schedule: Managed M2M Service Providers

417. Managed M2M Service Providers project work estimates Who is managing the work estimate quality of work tasks in the Managed M2M Service Providers project schedule?

418. Why is this particularly bad?

419. Why is software Managed M2M Service Providers project disaster so common?

420. Why do you need to manage Managed M2M Service Providers project Risk?

421. How can you address that situation?

422. Why or why not?

423. Activity charts and bar charts are graphical representations of a Managed M2M Service Providers project schedule ...how do they differ?

424. Are there activities that came from a template or previous Managed M2M Service Providers project that are not applicable on this phase of this Managed M2M Service Providers project?

425. How closely did the initial Managed M2M Service Providers project Schedule compare with the actual schedule?

426. What is risk?

427. To what degree is do you feel the entire team was committed to the Managed M2M Service Providers project schedule?

428. What documents, if any, will the subcontractor provide (eg Managed M2M Service Providers project schedule, quality plan etc)?

429. How can slack be negative?

430. What is the difference?

431. How can you minimize or control changes to Managed M2M Service Providers project schedules?

432. Are activities connected because logic dictates the order in which others occur?

433. Are key risk mitigation strategies added to the Managed M2M Service Providers project schedule?

434. Master Managed M2M Service Providers project schedule?

435. If you can not fix it, how do you do it differently?

2.20 Cost Management Plan: Managed M2M Service Providers

436. Are action items captured and managed?

437. How do you manage cost?

438. Milestones – what are the key dates in executing the contract plan?

439. Are key risk mitigation strategies added to the Managed M2M Service Providers project schedule?

440. Were stakeholders aware and supportive of the principles and practices of modern software estimation?

441. Are the Managed M2M Service Providers project plans updated on a frequent basis?

442. Was the scope definition used in task sequencing?

443. Are cause and effect determined for risks when others occur?

444. Time management – how will the schedule impact of changes be estimated and approved?

445. Have the procedures for identifying budget variances been followed?

446. Why do you manage cost?

447. Contingency rundown curve be used on the Managed M2M Service Providers project?

448. Progress measurement and control – How will the Managed M2M Service Providers project measure and control progress?

449. Are Managed M2M Service Providers project leaders committed to this Managed M2M Service Providers project full time?

450. Contractors scope – how will contractors scope be defined when contracts are let?

451. How difficult will it be to do specific tasks on the Managed M2M Service Providers project?

2.21 Activity Cost Estimates: Managed M2M Service Providers

452. What is the Managed M2M Service Providers projects sustainability strategy that will ensure Managed M2M Service Providers project results will endure or be sustained?

453. What makes a good expected result statement?

454. Were you satisfied with the work?

455. In which phase of the acquisition process cycle does source qualifications reside?

456. Were escalated issues resolved promptly?

457. One way to define activities is to consider how organization employees describe jobs to families and friends. You basically want to know, What do you do?

458. Can you delete activities or make them inactive?

459. Can you change your activities?

460. How many activities should you have?

461. How do you fund change orders?

462. The impact and what actions were taken?

463. How do you allocate indirect costs to activities?

464. Who determines the quality and expertise of contractors?

465. Were the costs or charges reasonable?

466. What procedures are put in place regarding bidding and cost comparisons, if any?

467. Is there anything unique in this Managed M2M Service Providers projects scope statement that will affect resources?

468. What happens if you cannot produce the documentation for the single audit?

469. Is costing method consistent with study goals?

470. How difficult will it be to do specific tasks on the Managed M2M Service Providers project?

471. Based on your Managed M2M Service Providers project communication management plan, what worked well?

2.22 Cost Estimating Worksheet: Managed M2M Service Providers

472. Is the Managed M2M Service Providers project responsive to community need?

473. What can be included?

474. What info is needed?

475. What is the estimated labor cost today based upon this information?

476. Ask: are others positioned to know, are others credible, and will others cooperate?

477. What is the purpose of estimating?

478. What costs are to be estimated?

479. What additional Managed M2M Service Providers project(s) could be initiated as a result of this Managed M2M Service Providers project?

480. Will the Managed M2M Service Providers project collaborate with the local community and leverage resources?

481. Identify the timeframe necessary to monitor progress and collect data to determine how the selected measure has changed?

482. What happens to any remaining funds not used?

483. What will others want?

484. How will the results be shared and to whom?

485. Is it feasible to establish a control group arrangement?

486. Does the Managed M2M Service Providers project provide innovative ways for stakeholders to overcome obstacles or deliver better outcomes?

487. Can a trend be established from historical performance data on the selected measure and are the criteria for using trend analysis or forecasting methods met?

488. Who is best positioned to know and assist in identifying corresponding factors?

2.23 Cost Baseline: Managed M2M Service Providers

489. Is the cr within Managed M2M Service Providers project scope?

490. Have all approved changes to the schedule baseline been identified and impact on the Managed M2M Service Providers project documented?

491. What would the life cycle costs be?

492. Definition of done can be traced back to the definitions of what are you providing to the customer in terms of deliverables?

493. Is there anything you need from upper management in order to be successful?

494. What does a good WBS NOT look like?

495. At which frequency ?

496. How accurate do cost estimates need to be?

497. What went right?

498. Have all approved changes to the Managed M2M Service Providers project requirement been identified and impact on the performance, cost, and schedule baselines documented?

499. Who will use corresponding metrics ?

500. Have the actual milestone completion dates been compared to the approved schedule?

501. What is the reality?

502. Has training and knowledge transfer of the operations organization been completed?

503. What is the most important thing to do next to make your Managed M2M Service Providers project successful?

504. What deliverables come first?

505. For what purpose ?

506. Are procedures defined by which the cost baseline may be changed?

507. What do you want to measure ?

2.24 Quality Management Plan: Managed M2M Service Providers

508. What would you gain if you spent time working to improve this process?

509. How is staff informed of proper reporting methods?

510. Who is approving the QAPP?

511. What key performance indicators does your organization use to measure, manage, and improve key processes?

512. What is the audience for the data?

513. How do you manage quality?

514. What process do you use to minimize errors, defects, and rework?

515. Does the program use modeling in the permitting or decision-making processes?

516. How does your organization determine the requirements and product/service features important to customers?

517. Were the right locations/samples tested for the right parameters?

518. Sampling part of task?

519. What field records are generated?

520. Have Managed M2M Service Providers project management standards and procedures been established and documented?

521. What are the established criteria that sampling / testing data are compared against?

522. How does your organization design processes to ensure others meet customer and others requirements?

523. How does your organization use comparative data and information to improve organizational performance?

524. Diagrams and tables to account for complex concepts and increase overall readability?

2.25 Quality Metrics: Managed M2M Service Providers

525. Can you correlate your quality metrics to profitability?

526. What is the timeline to meet your goal?

527. What do you measure?

528. How do you know if everyone is trying to improve the right things?

529. What does this tell us?

530. Do you stratify metrics by product or site?

531. Which data do others need in one place to target areas of improvement?

532. What method of measurement do you use?

533. How do you calculate corresponding metrics?

534. Filter visualizations of interest?

535. What about still open problems?

536. Who is willing to lead?

537. Is there a set of procedures to capture, analyze and act on quality metrics?

538. Which report did you use to create the data you are submitting?

539. Did the team meet the Managed M2M Service Providers project success criteria documented in the Quality Metrics Matrix?

540. Are there already quality metrics available that detect nonlinear embeddings and trends similar to the users perception?

541. Why is now the time for quality metrics?

542. What happens if you get an abnormal result?

543. What is the benchmark?

544. Where did complaints, returns and warranty claims come from?

2.26 Process Improvement Plan: Managed M2M Service Providers

545. Purpose of goal: the motive is determined by asking, why do you want to achieve this goal?

546. What personnel are the change agents for your initiative?

547. How do you measure?

548. Does your process ensure quality?

549. Are you following the quality standards?

550. Where do you want to be?

551. What is the test-cycle concept?

552. Who should prepare the process improvement action plan?

553. Why do you want to achieve the goal?

554. Has the time line required to move measurement results from the points of collection to databases or users been established?

555. To elicit goal statements, do you ask a question such as, What do you want to achieve?

556. What personnel are the coaches for your initiative?

557. Are there forms and procedures to collect and record the data?

558. What makes people good SPI coaches?

559. What actions are needed to address the problems and achieve the goals?

560. Where are you now?

561. Everyone agrees on what process improvement is, right?

562. Has a process guide to collect the data been developed?

563. Have the frequency of collection and the points in the process where measurements will be made been determined?

2.27 Responsibility Assignment Matrix: Managed M2M Service Providers

564. Do managers and team members provide helpful suggestions during review meetings?

565. Are the actual costs used for variance analysis reconcilable with data from the accounting system?

566. Is work properly classified as measured effort, LOE, or apportioned effort and appropriately separated?

567. When performing is split among two or more roles, is the work clearly defined so that the efforts are coordinated and the communication is clear?

568. Does each role with Accountable responsibility have the authority within your organization to make the required decisions?

569. Is budgeted cost for work performed calculated in a manner consistent with the way work is planned?

570. What are the deliverables?

571. Does the contractor use objective results, design reviews and tests to trace schedule performance?

572. Contemplated overhead expenditure for each period based on the best information currently available?

573. Are control accounts opened and closed based on the start and completion of work contained therein?

574. Is it safe to say you can handle more work or that some tasks you are supposed to do arent worth doing?

575. Incurrence of actual indirect costs in excess of budgets, by element of expense?

576. What simple tool can you use to help identify and prioritize Managed M2M Service Providers project risks that is very low tech and high touch?

577. Who is going to do that work?

578. Is work progressively subdivided into detailed work packages as requirements are defined?

579. Who is responsible for work and budgets for each wbs?

580. Are the wbs and organizational levels for application of the Managed M2M Service Providers projected overhead costs identified?

581. Changes in the current direct and Managed M2M Service Providers projected base?

2.28 Roles and Responsibilities: Managed M2M Service Providers

582. Is the data complete?

583. What expectations were NOT met?

584. Once the responsibilities are defined for the Managed M2M Service Providers project, have the deliverables, roles and responsibilities been clearly communicated to every participant?

585. Where are you most strong as a supervisor?

586. Attainable / achievable: the goal is attainable; can you actually accomplish the goal?

587. How well did the Managed M2M Service Providers project Team understand the expectations of specific roles and responsibilities?

588. Accountabilities: what are the roles and responsibilities of individual team members?

589. What specific behaviors did you observe?

590. Once the responsibilities are defined for the Managed M2M Service Providers project, have the deliverables, roles and responsibilities been clearly communicated to every participant?

591. Are governance roles and responsibilities documented?

592. Influence: what areas of organizational decision making are you able to influence when you do not have authority to make the final decision?

593. Be specific; avoid generalities. Thank you and great work alone are insufficient. What exactly do you appreciate and why?

594. Does your vision/mission support a culture of quality data?

595. Have you ever been a part of this team?

596. What is working well within your organizations performance management system?

597. How is your work-life balance?

598. Was the expectation clearly communicated?

599. What should you highlight for improvement?

2.29 Human Resource Management Plan: Managed M2M Service Providers

600. Is there a formal process for updating the Managed M2M Service Providers project baseline?

601. Are quality metrics defined?

602. Do you have the reasons why the changes to your organizational systems and capabilities are required?

603. Is there an issues management plan in place?

604. Are the quality tools and methods identified in the Quality Plan appropriate to the Managed M2M Service Providers project?

605. What are the Staffing Requirements?

606. Are assumptions being identified, recorded, analyzed, qualified and closed?

607. Are the right people being attracted and retained to meet the future challenges?

608. Are multiple estimation methods being employed?

609. Are actuals compared against estimates to analyze and correct variances?

610. Is documentation created for communication with the suppliers and Vendors?

611. Are vendor invoices audited for accuracy before payment?

612. Who needs training?

613. Are Managed M2M Service Providers project leaders committed to this Managed M2M Service Providers project full time?

614. Have all team members been part of identifying risks?

615. Are key risk mitigation strategies added to the Managed M2M Service Providers project schedule?

616. Is there a formal set of procedures supporting Stakeholder Management?

617. How to convince employees that this is a necessary process?

2.30 Communications Management Plan: Managed M2M Service Providers

618. Are there common objectives between the team and the stakeholder?

619. Do you ask; can you recommend others for you to talk with about this initiative?

620. Are others needed?

621. What help do you and your team need from the stakeholder?

622. What data is going to be required?

623. How often do you engage with stakeholders?

624. Who were proponents/opponents?

625. Who did you turn to if you had questions?

626. How is this initiative related to other portfolios, programs, or Managed M2M Service Providers projects?

627. Do you have members of your team responsible for certain stakeholders?

628. Will messages be directly related to the release strategy or phases of the Managed M2M Service Providers project?

629. How were corresponding initiatives successful?

630. Why is stakeholder engagement important?

631. Who are the members of the governing body?

632. Who will use or be affected by the result of a Managed M2M Service Providers project?

633. Who is involved as you identify stakeholders?

634. Which stakeholders are thought leaders, influences, or early adopters?

635. Are you constantly rushing from meeting to meeting?

636. What steps can you take for a positive relationship?

2.31 Risk Management Plan: Managed M2M Service Providers

637. How can you fix it?

638. Financial risk: can your organization afford to undertake the Managed M2M Service Providers project?

639. How will the Managed M2M Service Providers project know if your organizations risk response actions were effective?

640. Are requirements fully understood by the software engineering team and customers?

641. Was an original risk assessment/risk management plan completed?

642. My Managed M2M Service Providers project leader has suddenly left your organization, what do you do?

643. Are status updates being made on schedule and are the updates clearly described?

644. How is implementation of risk actions performed?

645. Why do you want risk management?

646. How is risk identification performed?

647. Is this an issue, action item, question or a risk?

648. Monitoring -what factors can you track that will enable you to determine if the risk is becoming more or less likely?

649. Are some people working on multiple Managed M2M Service Providers projects?

650. Is the customer technically sophisticated in the product area?

651. Mitigation -how can you avoid the risk?

652. Can the Managed M2M Service Providers project proceed without assuming the risk?

653. What should be done with non-critical risks?

654. Methodology: how will risk management be performed on this Managed M2M Service Providers project?

655. Are the software tools integrated with each other?

656. Degree of confidence in estimated size estimate?

2.32 Risk Register: Managed M2M Service Providers

657. How is a Community Risk Register created?

658. Risk probability and impact: how will the probabilities and impacts of risk items be assessed?

659. Cost/benefit – how much will the proposed mitigations cost and how does this cost compare with the potential cost of the risk event/situation should it occur?

660. Which key risks have ineffective responses or outstanding improvement actions?

661. What are you going to do to limit the Managed M2M Service Providers projects risk exposure due to the identified risks?

662. Can the likelihood and impact of failing to achieve corresponding recommendations and action plans be assessed?

663. How well are risks controlled?

664. What is your current and future risk profile?

665. What is the reason for current performance gaps and do the risks and opportunities identified previously account for this?

666. Preventative actions - planned actions to reduce

the likelihood a risk will occur and/or reduce the seriousness should it occur. What should you do now?

667. Assume the risk event or situation happens, what would the impact be?

668. Market risk -will the new service or product be useful to your organization or marketable to others?

669. Do you require further engagement?

670. User involvement: do you have the right users?

671. What may happen or not go according to plan?

672. What should you do when?

673. What risks might negatively or positively affect achieving the Managed M2M Service Providers project objectives?

674. Manageability – have mitigations to the risk been identified?

675. Recovery actions - planned actions taken once a risk has occurred to allow you to move on. What should you do after?

676. What would the impact to the Managed M2M Service Providers project objectives be should the risk arise?

2.33 Probability and Impact Assessment: Managed M2M Service Providers

677. Has something like this been done before?

678. What can you do about it?

679. Are formal technical reviews part of this process?

680. Monitoring of the overall Managed M2M Service Providers project status – are there any changes in the Managed M2M Service Providers project that can effect and cause new possible risks?

681. How do you maximize short-term return on investment?

682. What is the likely future demand of the customer?

683. What is the impact if the risk does occur?

684. Is the present organizational structure for handling the Managed M2M Service Providers project sufficient?

685. Risk urgency assessment -which of your risks could occur soon, or require a longer planning time?

686. How is the risk management process used in practice?

687. How are the local factors going to affect the absorption?

688. Are the risk data timely and relevant?

689. How will economic events and trends likely affect the Managed M2M Service Providers project?

690. Are some people working on multiple Managed M2M Service Providers projects?

691. How will the consumption pattern change?

692. Are flexibility and reuse paramount?

693. What risks are necessary to achieve success?

694. How are you working with risks?

695. What can you do to minimize the impact if it does?

696. Supply/demand Managed M2M Service Providers projections and trends; what are the levels of accuracy?

2.34 Probability and Impact Matrix: Managed M2M Service Providers

697. Which role do you have in the Managed M2M Service Providers project?

698. What are ways to measure and evaluate risks?

699. Premium on reliability of product?

700. Have you ascribed a level of confidence to every critical technical objective?

701. Should the risk be taken at all?

702. Have staff received necessary training?

703. Are team members trained in the use of the tools?

704. Are you on schedule?

705. What are the chances the risk events will occur?

706. Can you handle the investment risk?

707. Do the people have the right combinations of skills?

708. Brain storm – mind maps, what if?

709. Could others have been better mitigated?

710. What will the damage be?

711. What should you do FIRST?

712. Do you train all developers in the process?

713. Do you use any methods to analyze risks?

714. How would you suggest monitoring for risk transition indicators?

715. Do you have a mechanism for managing change?

716. Can the risk be avoided by choosing a different alternative?

2.35 Risk Data Sheet: Managed M2M Service Providers

717. What are the main threats to your existence?

718. What are you trying to achieve (Objectives)?

719. What are you here for (Mission)?

720. What can happen?

721. What can you do?

722. Will revised controls lead to tolerable risk levels?

723. How can it happen?

724. How do you handle product safely?

725. If it happens, what are the consequences?

726. Who has a vested interest in how you perform as your organization (our stakeholders)?

727. What will be the consequences if it happens?

728. What is the environment within which you operate (social trends, economic, community values, broad based participation, national directions etc.)?

729. What was measured?

730. What are your core values?

731. Potential for recurrence?

732. What will be the consequences if the risk happens?

733. Whom do you serve (customers)?

734. During work activities could hazards exist?

2.36 Procurement Management Plan: Managed M2M Service Providers

735. Managed M2M Service Providers project Objectives?

736. Are updated Managed M2M Service Providers project time & resource estimates reasonable based on the current Managed M2M Service Providers project stage?

737. Is there a procurement management plan in place?

738. Is Managed M2M Service Providers project work proceeding in accordance with the original Managed M2M Service Providers project schedule?

739. Are Managed M2M Service Providers project team roles and responsibilities identified and documented?

740. Are trade-offs between accepting the risk and mitigating the risk identified?

741. Does the resource management plan include a personnel development plan?

742. Have all documents been archived in a Managed M2M Service Providers project repository for each release?

743. If independent estimates will be needed as

evaluation criteria, who will prepare them and when?

744. Are metrics used to evaluate and manage Vendors?

745. Are the Managed M2M Service Providers project plans updated on a frequent basis?

746. If standardized procurement documents are needed, where can others be found?

747. Are milestone deliverables effectively tracked and compared to Managed M2M Service Providers project plan?

748. What communication items need improvement?

749. Have all unresolved risks been documented?

750. Are stakeholders aware and supportive of the principles and practices of modern software estimation?

751. Are meeting minutes captured and sent out after meetings?

752. What are your quality assurance overheads?

2.37 Source Selection Criteria: Managed M2M Service Providers

753. Do you want to have them collaborate at subfactor level?

754. Are responses to considerations adequate?

755. How should the preproposal conference be conducted?

756. How can the methods of publicizing the buy be tailored to yield more effective price competition?

757. Can you reasonably estimate total organization requirements for the coming year?

758. Is the offeror pricing what is technically proposed?

759. What instructions should be provided regarding oral presentations?

760. How do you facilitate evaluation against published criteria?

761. When and what information can be considered with offerors regarding past performance?

762. What evidence should be provided regarding proposal evaluations?

763. When should debriefings be held and how

should they be scheduled?

764. Does the evaluation of any change include an impact analysis; how will the change affect the scope, time, cost, and quality of the goods or services being provided?

765. In the technical/management area, what criteria do you use to determine the final evaluation ratings?

766. What information is to be provided and when should it be provided?

767. How should oral presentations be evaluated?

768. In order of importance, which evaluation criteria are the most critical to the determination of your overall rating?

769. How should oral presentations be prepared for?

770. Is the contracting office likely to receive more purchase requests for this item or service during the coming year?

771. Do you want to wait until all offerors have been evaluated?

2.38 Stakeholder Management Plan: Managed M2M Service Providers

772. Is the performance of the supplier to be rated and documented?

773. What procedures will be utilised to ensure effective monitoring of Managed M2M Service Providers project progress?

774. What is to be the method of release?

775. Are risk triggers captured?

776. Was trending evident between audits?

777. Are procurement deliverables arriving on time and to specification?

778. Are there standards for code development?

779. Are schedule deliverables actually delivered?

780. Does the Managed M2M Service Providers project have a Statement of Work?

781. What process was used to identify risks to the Managed M2M Service Providers projects success?

782. Is there general agreement & acceptance of the current status and progress of the Managed M2M Service Providers project?

783. How are you doing/what can be done better?

784. Have all involved stakeholders and work groups committed to the Managed M2M Service Providers project?

785. What is the general purpose in defining responsibilities of the already stated affiliated with the Managed M2M Service Providers project?

786. Has a quality assurance plan been developed for the Managed M2M Service Providers project?

787. Does this include subcontracted development?

788. Who is responsible for arranging and managing the review(s)?

789. Is there a requirements change management processes in place?

790. Does the Managed M2M Service Providers project have a formal Managed M2M Service Providers project Plan?

2.39 Change Management Plan: Managed M2M Service Providers

791. What new behaviours are required?

792. Who will be the change levers?

793. Has an information & communications plan been developed?

794. What is the most positive interpretation it can receive?

795. What are the training strategies?

796. What is the reason for the communication?

797. What do you expect the target audience to do, say, think or feel as a result of this communication?

798. Which relationships will change?

799. When does it make sense to customize?

800. Is there a software application relevant to this deliverable?

801. How might they respond to the message and if the response may be negative or open to misinterpretation, what else needs to be said?

802. What are the current methods of sharing information and do there need to be new ones

developed?

803. What work practices will be affected?

804. What time commitment will this involve?

805. What policies and procedures need to be changed?

806. Has this been negotiated with the customer and sponsor?

807. How much Managed M2M Service Providers project management is needed?

808. Do you need a new organizational structure?

809. What are the dependencies?

3.0 Executing Process Group: Managed M2M Service Providers

810. What will you do to minimize the impact should a risk event occur?

811. What Managed M2M Service Providers projects and services are in the portfolio of your organization?

812. What are the critical steps involved with strategy mapping?

813. Is the Managed M2M Service Providers project making progress in helping to achieve the set results?

814. How can you use Microsoft Managed M2M Service Providers project and Excel to assist in Managed M2M Service Providers project risk management?

815. Are escalated issues resolved promptly?

816. How do you measure difficulty?

817. What are the critical steps involved in selecting measures and initiatives?

818. How will professionals learn what is expected from them what the deliverables are?

819. How does the job market and current state of the economy affect human resource management?

820. If a risk event occurs, what will you do?

821. After how many days will the lease cost be the same as the purchase cost for the equipment?

822. How could you control progress of your Managed M2M Service Providers project?

823. Do the products created live up to the necessary quality?

824. It under budget or over budget?

825. What is in place for ensuring adequate change control on Managed M2M Service Providers projects that involve outside contracts?

826. What were things that you need to improve?

827. How does Managed M2M Service Providers project management relate to other disciplines?

828. What is the product of your Managed M2M Service Providers project?

3.1 Team Member Status Report: Managed M2M Service Providers

829. Does your organization have the means (staff, money, contract, etc.) to produce or to acquire the product, good, or service?

830. How will resource planning be done?

831. Will the staff do training or is that done by a third party?

832. Does the product, good, or service already exist within your organization?

833. When a teams productivity and success depend on collaboration and the efficient flow of information, what generally fails them?

834. How it is to be done?

835. Does every department have to have a Managed M2M Service Providers project Manager on staff?

836. Are your organizations Managed M2M Service Providers projects more successful over time?

837. What is to be done?

838. How does this product, good, or service meet the needs of the Managed M2M Service Providers project and your organization as a whole?

839. The problem with Reward & Recognition Programs is that the truly deserving people all too often get left out. How can you make it practical?

840. How can you make it practical?

841. Why is it to be done?

842. How much risk is involved?

843. Are the products of your organizations Managed M2M Service Providers projects meeting customers objectives?

844. What specific interest groups do you have in place?

845. Do you have an Enterprise Managed M2M Service Providers project Management Office (EPMO)?

846. Are the attitudes of staff regarding Managed M2M Service Providers project work improving?

847. Is there evidence that staff is taking a more professional approach toward management of your organizations Managed M2M Service Providers projects?

3.2 Change Request: Managed M2M Service Providers

848. Can you answer what happened, who did it, when did it happen, and what else will be affected?

849. What are the duties of the change control team?

850. What are the requirements for urgent changes?

851. For which areas does this operating procedure apply?

852. What is the function of the change control committee?

853. Has your address changed?

854. How does a team identify the discrete elements of a configuration?

855. Are there requirements attributes that are strongly related to the occurrence of defects and failures?

856. Are change requests logged and managed?

857. What type of changes does change control take into account?

858. What needs to be communicated?

859. When do you create a change request?

860. How does your organization control changes before and after software is released to a customer?

861. Will all change requests and current status be logged?

862. Who can suggest changes?

863. What is the purpose of change control?

864. How well do experienced software developers predict software change?

865. Who is responsible to authorize changes?

866. What is the relationship between requirements attributes and attributes like complexity and size?

3.3 Change Log: Managed M2M Service Providers

867. Is the submitted change a new change or a modification of a previously approved change?

868. Who initiated the change request?

869. Is the requested change request a result of changes in other Managed M2M Service Providers project(s)?

870. Will the Managed M2M Service Providers project fail if the change request is not executed?

871. How does this change affect the timeline of the schedule?

872. When was the request approved?

873. Does the suggested change request seem to represent a necessary enhancement to the product?

874. Where do changes come from?

875. How does this change affect scope?

876. When was the request submitted?

877. Is the change request open, closed or pending?

878. How does this relate to the standards developed for specific business processes?

879. Is this a mandatory replacement?

880. Should a more thorough impact analysis be conducted?

881. Is the change request within Managed M2M Service Providers project scope?

882. Is the change backward compatible without limitations?

883. Does the suggested change request represent a desired enhancement to the products functionality?

884. Do the described changes impact on the integrity or security of the system?

3.4 Decision Log: Managed M2M Service Providers

885. It becomes critical to track and periodically revisit both operational effectiveness; Are you noticing all that you need to, and are you interpreting what you see effectively?

886. Who will be given a copy of this document and where will it be kept?

887. Do strategies and tactics aimed at less than full control reduce the costs of management or simply shift the cost burden?

888. At what point in time does loss become unacceptable?

889. What is your overall strategy for quality control / quality assurance procedures?

890. Does anything need to be adjusted?

891. What is the line where eDiscovery ends and document review begins?

892. How does provision of information, both in terms of content and presentation, influence acceptance of alternative strategies?

893. How does an increasing emphasis on cost containment influence the strategies and tactics used?

894. Which variables make a critical difference?

895. What alternatives/risks were considered?

896. Is your opponent open to a non-traditional workflow, or will it likely challenge anything you do?

897. Meeting purpose; why does this team meet?

898. Adversarial environment. is your opponent open to a non-traditional workflow, or will it likely challenge anything you do?

899. What makes you different or better than others companies selling the same thing?

900. Linked to original objective?

901. How consolidated and comprehensive a story can you tell by capturing currently available incident data in a central location and through a log of key decisions during an incident?

902. What are the cost implications?

903. Is everything working as expected?

904. Decision-making process; how will the team make decisions?

3.5 Quality Audit: Managed M2M Service Providers

905. How does your organization ensure that equipment is appropriately maintained and producing valid results?

906. Are the review comments incorporated?

907. How are you auditing your organizations compliance with regulations?

908. Are the intentions consistent with external obligations (such as applicable laws)?

909. Is quality audit a prerequisite for program accreditation or program recognition?

910. How does your organization know that its public relations and marketing systems are appropriately effective and constructive?

911. How does your organization know that its management system is appropriately effective and constructive?

912. How does your organization know that its range of activities are being reviewed as rigorously and constructively as they could be?

913. How does the organization know that its industry and community engagement planning and management systems are appropriately effective

and constructive in enabling relationships with key stakeholder groups?

914. Health and safety arrangements; stress management workshops. How does your organization know that it provides a safe and healthy environment?

915. Have personnel cleanliness and health requirements been established?

916. Are multiple statements on the same issue consistent with each other?

917. How does your organization know that its systems for communicating with and among staff are appropriately effective and constructive?

918. Are salvageable and salvaged medical devices stored in a manner to prevent damage and/or contamination?

919. How do staff know if they are doing a good job?

920. How does your organization know that its system for inducting new staff to maximize workplace contributions are appropriately effective and constructive?

921. How does your organization know that its system for recruiting the best staff possible are appropriately effective and constructive?

922. Are all complaints involving the possible failure of a device, labeling, or packaging to meet any of its specifications reviewed, evaluated, and investigated?

923. Is there any content that may be legally actionable?

924. How does your organization know that its staff are presenting original work, and properly acknowledging the work of others?

3.6 Team Directory: Managed M2M Service Providers

925. Is construction on schedule?

926. How does the team resolve conflicts and ensure tasks are completed?

927. Decisions: is the most suitable form of contract being used?

928. When does information need to be distributed?

929. Who will report Managed M2M Service Providers project status to all stakeholders?

930. Days from the time the issue is identified?

931. Have you decided when to celebrate the Managed M2M Service Providers projects completion date?

932. Process decisions: do invoice amounts match accepted work in place?

933. Decisions: what could be done better to improve the quality of the constructed product?

934. Does a Managed M2M Service Providers project team directory list all resources assigned to the Managed M2M Service Providers project?

935. Who is the Sponsor?

936. Timing: when do the effects of communication take place?

937. Process decisions: how well was task order work performed?

938. Who are the Team Members?

939. How and in what format should information be presented?

940. Why is the work necessary?

941. How will the team handle changes?

942. Where will the product be used and/or delivered or built when appropriate?

943. When will you produce deliverables?

3.7 Team Operating Agreement: Managed M2M Service Providers

944. Do you brief absent members after they view meeting notes or listen to a recording?

945. Reimbursements: how will the team members be reimbursed for expenses and time commitments?

946. How does teaming fit in with overall organizational goals and meet organizational needs?

947. Do you solicit member feedback about meetings and what would make them better?

948. What is the anticipated procedure (recruitment, solicitation of volunteers, or assignment) for selecting team members?

949. To whom do you deliver your services?

950. Have you established procedures that team members can follow to work effectively together, such as a team operating agreement?

951. Did you draft the meeting agenda?

952. Have you set the goals and objectives of the team?

953. Do you prevent individuals from dominating the meeting?

954. Are team roles clearly defined and accepted?

955. Do you send out the agenda and meeting materials in advance?

956. Do you post meeting notes and the recording (if used) and notify participants?

957. Do you call or email participants to ensure understanding, follow-through and commitment to the meeting outcomes?

958. How do you want to be thought of and known within your organization?

959. Resource allocation: how will individual team members account for time and expenses, and how will this be allocated in the team budget?

960. Seconds for members to respond?

961. How will your group handle planned absences?

962. What types of accommodations will be formulated and put in place for sustaining the team?

963. What is teaming?

3.8 Team Performance Assessment: Managed M2M Service Providers

964. Is there a particular method of data analysis that you would recommend as a means of demonstrating that method variance is not of great concern for a given dataset?

965. To what degree are the skill areas critical to team performance present?

966. How hard do you try to make a good selection?

967. How does Managed M2M Service Providers project termination impact Managed M2M Service Providers project team members?

968. To what degree are the relative importance and priority of the goals clear to all team members?

969. To what degree will the team ensure that all members equitably share the work essential to the success of the team?

970. To what degree does the teams work approach provide opportunity for members to engage in fact-based problem solving?

971. To what degree will the approach capitalize on and enhance the skills of all team members in a manner that takes into consideration other demands on members of the team?

972. To what degree are the goals realistic?

973. When does the medium matter?

974. Lack of method variance in self-reported affect and perceptions at work: Reality or artifact?

975. Delaying market entry: how long is too long?

976. Individual task proficiency and team process behavior: what is important for team functioning?

977. To what degree are the members clear on what they are individually responsible for and what they are jointly responsible for?

978. To what degree can team members meet frequently enough to accomplish the teams ends?

979. To what degree do team members feel that the purpose of the team is important, if not exciting?

980. If you have received criticism from reviewers that your work suffered from method variance, what was the circumstance?

981. What do you think is the most constructive thing that could be done now to resolve considerations and disputes about method variance?

982. What are you doing specifically to develop the leaders around you?

983. To what degree does the teams work approach provide opportunity for members to engage in results-based evaluation?

3.9 Team Member Performance Assessment: Managed M2M Service Providers

984. How do you use data to inform instruction and improve staff achievement?

985. How will they be formed?

986. Are any validation activities performed?

987. How does your team work together?

988. Who is responsible?

989. Are assessment validation activities performed?

990. What future plans (e.g., modifications) do you have for your program?

991. Does the rater (supervisor) have the authority or responsibility to tell an employee that the employees performance is unsatisfactory?

992. What stakeholders must be involved in the development and oversight of the performance plan?

993. What are the standards or expectations for success?

994. How do you implement Cost Reduction?

995. To what degree do the goals specify concrete

team work products?

996. What happens if a team member disagrees with the Job Expectations?

997. What are acceptable governance changes?

998. Is it critical or vital to the job?

999. To what degree do all members feel responsible for all agreed-upon measures?

1000. Are there any safeguards to prevent intentional or unintentional rating errors?

1001. To what degree does the teams purpose contain themes that are particularly meaningful and memorable?

3.10 Issue Log: Managed M2M Service Providers

1002. How do you reply to this question; you am new here and managing this major program. How do you suggest you build your network?

1003. How do you manage communications?

1004. Why do you manage communications?

1005. Is there an important stakeholder who is actively opposed and will not receive messages?

1006. What help do you and your team need from the stakeholders?

1007. Are the stakeholders getting the information they need, are they consulted, are concerns addressed?

1008. Who needs to know and how much?

1009. Are there too many who have an interest in some aspect of your work?

1010. Do you feel a register helps?

1011. Which team member will work with each stakeholder?

1012. How do you manage human resources?

1013. Where do team members get information?

1014. Are there potential barriers between the team and the stakeholder?

1015. Who reported the issue?

1016. Can you think of other people who might have concerns or interests?

1017. In classifying stakeholders, which approach to do so are you using?

1018. Persistence; will users learn a work around or will they be bothered every time?

1019. What would have to change?

4.0 Monitoring and Controlling Process Group: Managed M2M Service Providers

1020. Is there adequate validation on required fields?

1021. Did you implement the program as designed?

1022. Did it work?

1023. How was the program set-up initiated?

1024. How many potential communications channels exist on the Managed M2M Service Providers project?

1025. Did the Managed M2M Service Providers project team have the right skills?

1026. Specific - is the objective clear in terms of what, how, when, and where the situation will be changed?

1027. What resources (both financial and non-financial) are available/needed?

1028. Is the verbiage used appropriate and understandable?

1029. What are the goals of the program?

1030. Where is the Risk in the Managed M2M Service Providers project?

1031. Are there areas that need improvement?

1032. Based on your Managed M2M Service Providers project communication management plan, what worked well?

1033. Were decisions made in a timely manner?

1034. How is agile program management done?

1035. Does the solution fit in with organizations technical architectural requirements?

1036. How to ensure validity, quality and consistency?

1037. How is agile Managed M2M Service Providers project management done?

1038. How can you make your needs known?

1039. Measurable - are the targets measurable?

4.1 Project Performance Report: Managed M2M Service Providers

1040. To what degree is there a sense that only the team can succeed?

1041. To what degree can the cognitive capacity of individuals accommodate the flow of information?

1042. To what degree do individual skills and abilities match task demands?

1043. To what degree does the information network communicate information relevant to the task?

1044. To what degree will the team adopt a concrete, clearly understood, and agreed-upon approach that will result in achievement of the teams goals?

1045. To what degree are sub-teams possible or necessary?

1046. To what degree do the relationships of the informal organization motivate taskrelevant behavior and facilitate task completion?

1047. How will procurement be coordinated with other Managed M2M Service Providers project aspects, such as scheduling and performance reporting?

1048. To what degree do team members agree with the goals, relative importance, and the ways in which achievement will be measured?

1049. To what degree will each member have the opportunity to advance his or her professional skills in all three of the above categories while contributing to the accomplishment of the teams purpose and goals?

1050. To what degree are the demands of the task compatible with and converge with the mission and functions of the formal organization?

1051. What is the PRS?

1052. To what degree can the team measure progress against specific goals?

1053. To what degree can the team ensure that all members are individually and jointly accountable for the teams purpose, goals, approach, and work-products?

4.2 Variance Analysis: Managed M2M Service Providers

1054. Are indirect costs accumulated for comparison with the corresponding budgets?

1055. Is there a logical explanation for any variance?

1056. What is the actual cost of work performed?

1057. What are the direct labor dollars and/or hours?

1058. Do work packages consist of discrete tasks which are adequately described?

1059. There are detailed schedules which support control account and work package start and completion dates/events?

1060. Are overhead costs budgets established on a basis consistent with the anticipated direct business base?

1061. The anticipated business volume?

1062. Are data elements reconcilable between internal summary reports and reports forwarded to the stakeholders?

1063. Other relevant issues of Variance Analysis -selling price or gross margin?

1064. Are all cwbs elements specified for external

reporting?

1065. Are records maintained to show how undistributed budgets are controlled?

1066. What are the actual costs to date?

1067. What does an unfavorable overhead volume variance mean?

1068. What is exceptional?

1069. Why do variances exist?

1070. Are overhead cost budgets established for each department which has authority to incur overhead costs?

1071. Who are responsible for the establishment of budgets and assignment of resources for overhead performance?

1072. What is the incurrence of actual indirect costs in excess of budgets, by element of expense?

4.3 Earned Value Status: Managed M2M Service Providers

1073. What is the unit of forecast value?

1074. Verification is a process of ensuring that the developed system satisfies the stakeholders agreements and specifications; Are you building the product right? What do you verify?

1075. Where is evidence-based earned value in your organization reported?

1076. Validation is a process of ensuring that the developed system will actually achieve the stakeholders desired outcomes; Are you building the right product? What do you validate?

1077. Are you hitting your Managed M2M Service Providers projects targets?

1078. Earned value can be used in almost any Managed M2M Service Providers project situation and in almost any Managed M2M Service Providers project environment. it may be used on large Managed M2M Service Providers projects, medium sized Managed M2M Service Providers projects, tiny Managed M2M Service Providers projects (in cut-down form), complex and simple Managed M2M Service Providers projects and in any market sector. some people, of course, know all about earned value, they have used it for years - but perhaps not as effectively as they could have?

1079. If earned value management (EVM) is so good in determining the true status of a Managed M2M Service Providers project and Managed M2M Service Providers project its completion, why is it that hardly any one uses it in information systems related Managed M2M Service Providers projects?

1080. Where are your problem areas?

1081. How does this compare with other Managed M2M Service Providers projects?

1082. When is it going to finish?

1083. How much is it going to cost by the finish?

4.4 Risk Audit: Managed M2M Service Providers

1084. To what extent are auditors effective at linking business risks and management assertions?

1085. What impact does prior experience have on decisions made during the risk-assessment process?

1086. What effect would a better risk management program have had?

1087. Are procedures in place to ensure the security of staff and information and compliance with privacy legislation if applicable?

1088. How effective are your risk controls?

1089. Does the Managed M2M Service Providers project team have experience with the technology to be implemented?

1090. Have all involved been advised of any obligations they have to sponsors?

1091. Is all expenditure authorised through an identified process?

1092. Are risk management strategies documented?

1093. Does your organization have or has considered the need for insurance covers: public liability, professional indemnity and directors and officers liability?

1094. Do you manage the process through use of metrics?

1095. Does your organization have a social media policy and procedure?

1096. Should additional substantive testing be conducted because of the risk audit results?

1097. Management -what contingency plans do you have if the risk becomes a reality?

1098. Is there a clear procedure for reporting accidents/injuries?

1099. Is a software Managed M2M Service Providers project management tool available?

1100. What are risks and how do you manage them?

1101. Is the customer willing to establish rapid communication links with the developer?

1102. Do you have position descriptions for all office bearers/staff?

4.5 Contractor Status Report: Managed M2M Service Providers

1103. Who can list a Managed M2M Service Providers project as organization experience, your organization or a previous employee of your organization?

1104. What process manages the contracts?

1105. How is risk transferred?

1106. What are the minimum and optimal bandwidth requirements for the proposed solution?

1107. What was the final actual cost?

1108. Describe how often regular updates are made to the proposed solution. Are corresponding regular updates included in the standard maintenance plan?

1109. What was the budget or estimated cost for your organizations services?

1110. Are there contractual transfer concerns?

1111. What is the average response time for answering a support call?

1112. What was the overall budget or estimated cost?

1113. How does the proposed individual meet each requirement?

1114. How long have you been using the services?

1115. What was the actual budget or estimated cost for your organizations services?

1116. If applicable; describe your standard schedule for new software version releases. Are new software version releases included in the standard maintenance plan?

4.6 Formal Acceptance: Managed M2M Service Providers

1117. Was business value realized?

1118. How does your team plan to obtain formal acceptance on your Managed M2M Service Providers project?

1119. Was the Managed M2M Service Providers project goal achieved?

1120. What are the requirements against which to test, Who will execute?

1121. Who would use it?

1122. What can you do better next time?

1123. Does it do what client said it would?

1124. Was the sponsor/customer satisfied?

1125. What was done right?

1126. Do you perform formal acceptance or burn-in tests?

1127. Is formal acceptance of the Managed M2M Service Providers project product documented and distributed?

1128. Who supplies data?

1129. How well did the team follow the methodology?

1130. Have all comments been addressed?

1131. What features, practices, and processes proved to be strengths or weaknesses?

1132. What is the Acceptance Management Process?

1133. Did the Managed M2M Service Providers project achieve its MOV?

1134. Was the Managed M2M Service Providers project managed well?

1135. Does it do what Managed M2M Service Providers project team said it would?

1136. Do you buy pre-configured systems or build your own configuration?

5.0 Closing Process Group: Managed M2M Service Providers

1137. Are there funding or time constraints?

1138. Who are the Managed M2M Service Providers project stakeholders?

1139. Did the Managed M2M Service Providers project team have the right skills?

1140. Does the close educate others to improve performance?

1141. What were the actual outcomes?

1142. What is the overall risk of the Managed M2M Service Providers project to your organization?

1143. What were things that you did very well and want to do the same again on the next Managed M2M Service Providers project?

1144. Did you do things well?

1145. How well did the team follow the chosen processes?

1146. What areas were overlooked on this Managed M2M Service Providers project?

1147. What is the Managed M2M Service Providers project name and date of completion?

1148. Is this an updated Managed M2M Service Providers project Proposal Document?

1149. How critical is the Managed M2M Service Providers project success to the success of your organization?

1150. What went well?

1151. What is the Managed M2M Service Providers project Management Process?

1152. Were the outcomes different from the already stated planned?

5.1 Procurement Audit: Managed M2M Service Providers

1153. Do the buyers always select or authorize the source of supply on other than contract purchases?

1154. Does an appropriately qualified official check the quality of performance against the contract terms?

1155. Are there authorizations on file to support all deductions from payroll checks?

1156. Was suitability of candidates accurately assessed?

1157. Were no tenders presented after the time limit accepted?

1158. Is your organization aware and informed about international procurement standards and good practice?

1159. Has it been determined which areas of procurement the audit should cover?

1160. Was the award decision based on the result of the evaluation of tenders?

1161. Was the tender clearly and properly specified, including evaluation criteria and knowing about the market and therefore not over-prescriptive and receptive to innovation?

1162. Are all purchase orders accounted for?

1163. Did your organization state the minimum requirements to be met by the variants in the tender documents?

1164. Does the procurement unit have sound commercial awareness and knowledge of suppliers and the market?

1165. Was the estimated contract value in line with the final cost of the contract awarded?

1166. Was the estimated contract value based on realistic and updated prices?

1167. Does the strategy ensure that needs are met, and not exceeded?

1168. Are payment generated from computer programs reviewed by supervisory personnel prior to distribution?

1169. Were there no material changes in the contract shortly after award?

1170. Does the department evaluate and benchmark the performance of the procurement function/ unit against other comparable procurement functions/ units?

1171. Is the relationship between in-house and external work considered in the strategy?

1172. Is the purchasing department consulted on

favorable purchasing opportunities, economic ordering quantities, and revision of purchasing specifications?

5.2 Contract Close-Out: Managed M2M Service Providers

1173. Why Outsource?

1174. Has each contract been audited to verify acceptance and delivery?

1175. Was the contract type appropriate?

1176. Have all acceptance criteria been met prior to final payment to contractors?

1177. What is capture management?

1178. Change in attitude or behavior?

1179. Change in knowledge?

1180. Are the signers the authorized officials?

1181. How is the contracting office notified of the automatic contract close-out?

1182. How/when used ?

1183. Parties: who is involved?

1184. Have all contracts been completed?

1185. Have all contract records been included in the Managed M2M Service Providers project archives?

1186. How does it work?

1187. Was the contract sufficiently clear so as not to result in numerous disputes and misunderstandings?

1188. Change in circumstances?

1189. Have all contracts been closed?

1190. Was the contract complete without requiring numerous changes and revisions?

1191. Parties: Authorized?

1192. What happens to the recipient of services?

5.3 Project or Phase Close-Out: Managed M2M Service Providers

1193. Is there a clear cause and effect between the activity and the lesson learned?

1194. Who is responsible for award close-out?

1195. What is a Risk Management Process?

1196. Were risks identified and mitigated?

1197. What is the information level of detail required for each stakeholder?

1198. What were the desired outcomes?

1199. In addition to assessing whether the Managed M2M Service Providers project was successful, it is equally critical to analyze why it was or was not fully successful. Are you including this?

1200. What are the informational communication needs for each stakeholder?

1201. Have business partners been involved extensively, and what data was required for them?

1202. What was the preferred delivery mechanism?

1203. Were cost budgets met?

1204. What hierarchical authority does the

stakeholder have in your organization?

1205. Does the lesson educate others to improve performance?

1206. Who exerted influence that has positively affected or negatively impacted the Managed M2M Service Providers project?

1207. If you were the Managed M2M Service Providers project sponsor, how would you determine which Managed M2M Service Providers project team(s) and/ or individuals deserve recognition?

1208. What was expected from each stakeholder?

1209. In preparing the Lessons Learned report, should it reflect a consensus viewpoint, or should the report reflect the different individual viewpoints?

1210. Did the delivered product meet the specified requirements and goals of the Managed M2M Service Providers project?

1211. Planned remaining costs?

1212. When and how were information needs best met?

5.4 Lessons Learned: Managed M2M Service Providers

1213. How clearly defined were the objectives for this Managed M2M Service Providers project?

1214. What were the challenges and pitfalls?

1215. How many interest groups are stakeholders?

1216. What are the expectations of the individuals?

1217. What is the expected lifespan of the deliverable?

1218. What were the key issues?

1219. What is your working hypothesis, if you have one?

1220. What needs to be done over or differently?

1221. How much of your time was spent on other than this Managed M2M Service Providers project?

1222. Do you conduct the engineering tests?

1223. Was sufficient advance training conducted and/or information provided to enable the already stated affected by the changes to adjust to and accommodate them?

1224. Where do you go from here?

1225. Who had fiscal authority to manage the funding for the Managed M2M Service Providers project, did that work?

1226. What did you do right?

1227. What is the supervisor to staff ratio?

1228. How smooth do you feel Integration has been?

1229. How effective were the techniques used to prepare you and your organization for the impact of the changes brought about by the product or service produced by the Managed M2M Service Providers project?

1230. How timely was the training you received in preparation for the use of the product/service?

1231. What is the value of the deliverable?

1232. Was sufficient time allocated to review Managed M2M Service Providers project deliverables?

Index

CPSIA information can be obtained
at www.ICGtesting.com
Printed in the USA
BVHW082019110819
555624BV00016BA/1843/P